KU-485-634

The Heritage of Literature Series
SECTION B NO. 10

MODERN ESSAYS

The Heritage of Literature Series
General Editor: E. W. Parker, M.C.

This series incorporates titles under the following headings: Travel and Adventure, Animal Stories, Fiction, Modern Classics, Short Stories, Prose Writing, Drama, Myths and Legends, Poetry.

Each title in the series falls into one of three main sections:

Section A, without notes;
Section B, with introduction and notes suitable for intensive study;
Section J, for younger readers.

Other titles in the Prose Writing section of the series include:

B.86 PROSE OF TODAY
B.53 TWENTIETH CENTURY PROSE, 1940-1960
B.25 THE ART OF THE ESSAYIST

A complete list of the series is available on request.

Catherine   Montgomery Q4
Colum MacPhee   B4.

PORTREE HIGH SCHOOL

Modern Essays

Selected with an Introduction by
A. C. WARD

LONGMANS

LONGMANS, GREEN AND CO LTD
48 Grosvenor Street, London W1

Associated companies, branches and representatives
throughout the world

This edition © Longmans, Green and Co Ltd 1968

PRINTED IN GREAT BRITAIN BY
NORTHUMBERLAND PRESS LIMITED
GATESHEAD

CONTENTS

vi CONTENTS

Science—Manufacture—Invention

Writers and Readers

Other Creatures

ACKNOWLEDGMENTS

We are grateful to the following for permission to reproduce copyright material :

Miss Sonia Brownell and Secker & Warburg Ltd. for 'Why I Write' from *Collected Essays* by George Orwell; author and author's agents for 'A Holiday In Time' by Sir Arthur Bryant from *Historians's Holiday*; The Bodley Head for 'The Case of the 1,251 Beards' from *Idly Oddly* by Paul Jennings (Max Reinhardt, Ltd., 1959); author and author's agents for 'Seas of Tomorrow' from *Voices in the Sky* by Arthur C. Clarke; Chatto & Windus Ltd. for 'The Birds of St James's' from *An Ideal Voyage* by Sir John Shuckburgh; Sir Robin Darwin for 'The Spirit of Picnic' from *Every Idle Dream* by Bernard Darwin; Alistair Cooke for 'It's a Democracy, Isn't It?' from *Letters from America* (Rupert Hart-Davis Ltd., 1951); Faber & Faber Ltd. for 'Billy the Kid' from *The Hot Gates* by William Golding and for 'Scotties' from *A Peck of Gold* by Alison Uttley; Kevin FitzGerald for his essay 'Death of the Business Letter' printed in *The Listener*, 2 May 1963; Robert Graves and Cassell & Co. Ltd. and author's agent for 'The Poet and His Public' by Robert Graves from *The Crowning Privilege*; proprietors of *The Guardian* for 'Guides to Dreamland' by John Laycock from *The Bedside Guardian 14*, 1965; Hamish Hamilton for 'The Boyhood of Fabre' from *Purely for Pleasure* by Margaret Lane; William Heinemann Ltd. for 'Litter Bugs' from *A Stroll Before Dark* by Richard Church and for 'The Newsvendor' from *The Other Half* by Hunter Davies; Sir Alan Herbert and Methuen & Co. Ltd. for 'Members' Pay' from *Bardot M.P.* by Sir Alan Herbert; author and author's agent for 'Apart, Not Together' by Penelope Mortimer; Sir Harold Nicolson for 'The Future of the Public Schools' from *Friday Mornings* by Sir Harold Nicolson; author and author's agent for 'Josiah Wedgwood' from *Men and Places* by J. H. Plumb; author and author's agent for 'Student Mobs' from *The Moments* by J. B. Priestley; Routledge & Kegan Paul Ltd. for 'Vulgarity' from *A Coat of Many Colours* by Sir Herbert Read; Norman Turner for his essay 'The Month for Spo' from the *B.B.C. Book of the Countryside* (1963); Mrs. Christine Orton and the proprietors of *The Times* for 'A Queen of Music' by Mrs. Orton, printed in *The Times* of 28 February 1966.

INTRODUCTION

IN THE present century of headlong change, when everything is now, or seems, different from what it was in 1900, literature in all its forms has developed along new lines. The poetry of T. S. Eliot and his successors is unlike that of, say, Tennyson and Swinburne; the plays of John Osborne, Arnold Wesker and their contemporaries are unlike those of Bernard Shaw or Noel Coward; the novels of James Joyce and Virginia Woolf unlike those of H. G. Wells or Rose Macaulay.

The essays in the present volume were all first published either in book form or in periodicals between 1940 and 1966, and the general tone of the volume is different from the tone of previous books of essays selected for the Heritage of Literature series.

Until these later years, essays published from the time the form began—in the sixteenth century, with Montaigne's *Essais* in France and with Bacon's *Essays* in England—could be grouped in two main classes which we may call (*a*) the *Formal* and (*b*) the *Familiar*: Formal essays those concerned with facts and information or with philosophical truths, Familiar essays roaming at large over anything and everything that interested the writer at the moment or that happened to come into his mind at the second his pen touched paper.

But whether formal or familiar, the essay had usually been marked by an intentionally *literary* quality in which close attention was given to the *manner* of expression, sometimes even more than to whether the matter was important or unimportant. The most impressive essayists, of course, gave equivalent importance to matter and manner. Thus, Francis Bacon's essays are formal and

ix

often profound in subject, but what they express stays in readers' minds mainly by means of the author's manner of expression, and often through epigrams so phrased that they are memorable as much because of the pleasing sound the words make as by the wisdom they expound: 'Read not to contradict and confute, nor to believe and take for granted, nor to find talk and discourse, but to weigh and consider'—a famous sentence from his essay 'Of Studies'.

Essays of both kinds—formal and familiar—came from various authors in the seventeenth and eighteenth centuries, but the Familiar essay reached its peak in Charles Lamb's *Essays of Elia* in the 1820s. Lamb became the model for a number of writers in the early part of the twentieth century, particularly for E. V. Lucas and Robert Lynd, whose essays are represented in the earlier volumes of this series. Lamb, Lucas, and Lynd were happy with such essay subjects as 'A Dissertation upon Roast Pig', 'Those Thirty Minutes' (on the embarrassments of being 'seen off' by friends or relatives on railway station platforms), or 'Eggs: An Easter Homily'. Such subjects can be treated with playful humour, mock seriousness, or frivolity, or be sentimental or whimsical or outright comic.

While the two categories of essays are usually wide apart in subject, all their writers would have agreed that how they wrote was no less important than what they wrote about. They were all conscious of *style* as well as of subject. There is no hard and fast formula for literary style, and it is as true now that 'style is the man himself' (*Le style est l'homme même*) as it was when the French scientist, Buffon, said it in the eighteenth century. He meant that every writer's or artist's style reflects the creator's own personality and differs from all others.

Nevertheless, essay writers, even the 'familiar' ones, were accustomed to observe certain formalities of prose style—order and dignity, eloquence, harmony and grace. Because of these customary observances, essays were at one time catalogued under the general heading *belles lettres*, interpreted as 'polite literature' and appealing especially to readers who valued good manners both in literature and in life.

We can add an important rider to Buffon's definition that 'style is the man himself', and say that 'style is the man himself *in the society of his own time*'. Though some writers prefer solitude to society, John Donne rightly believed that 'No man is an Island, entire of itself; every man is a piece of the Continent'; for each of us that continent is the society in which we live and which shapes us even if, individually, we rebel against it.

Whether we like it or not, whether we revolt against it or not, we cannot but recognize that the society in which we have lived since 1939 is not a society in which 'polite literature' could flourish.

In Bernard Shaw's play *The Apple Cart*, King Magnus tells Orinthia that 'without good manners human society is intolerable and impossible'. That was said in 1929. Since then society has chosen to get along on a basis of bad manners in every walk of life, from international politics to football. Here, this is a fact to record, not a phenomenon to moralize about or bemoan. It is a fact to record in explanation of the absence from some at least of the essays in this book of what earlier writers and readers would have admired as Style. Then, the Art of Writing would have appeared important, but latterly more publicity has been given to 'anti-art', and a good deal of literature has been put into jeans and duffle coats instead of elegant attire.

We can drop the metaphor and account for the change in English prose style (with a small 's') by noting that there has been in literature a progression, or perhaps a regression, from literary English to spoken English—literary English having come to be regarded as artificial, spoken English as natural. Therefore, no doubt often unconsciously directed by 'the spirit of the age' rather than by any conscious striving to conform to current fashion, writers have tended to become more colloquial and to write as they would speak.

While this trend is in line with the throwing off of polite (i.e. formal) manners in society at large, it has been greatly accelerated by radio broadcasting, in which the spoken word must prevail over the written word. Broadcasters only rarely deliver essays or lectures. They give talks. Whereas past generations would have been shocked by authors who consistently wrote in the relaxed English that we commonly speak, now we should be bored and switch off broadcasters who spoke as their grandfathers wrote, or even as their grandfathers talked. Each generation speaks in its own idiom, though ours is the first generation that has deliberately aimed to write in its own spoken idiom.

Whether it be true or not that bad invariably drives out good, there is no doubt whatever that broadcasting has had a profound and probably ineffaceable influence on literature. So far as the essay is concerned, radio has very frequently become the channel of first publication. In the past, essays were first published (either in books or in periodicals) to limited numbers of readers; now they can be first published to millions of listeners before getting into print and made permanent. A few of the pieces in the present volume were first broadcast and only afterwards printed.

Furthermore, the merging of essays and talks has also broken down any barriers that may previously have existed between essays and 'articles', between essays and dialogues, between essays and interviews and tape-recordings. 'Guides to Dreamland' in this book is no less an essay for having been printed as a newspaper article in *The Guardian*; 'Members' Pay' is no less an essay for being cast in the shape of a fanciful legal judgment; 'The Newsvendor' no less an essay (or a Character, as such a piece would have been called in the seventeenth century) for being the report of a personal interview and employing the technique if not the actual instrument of a tape-recording.

The essay is too varied and hospitable a kind of writing to allow an anthology to be confined to a common or uniform theme. Most of the essays here are linked only by some concern with human behaviour, while a proportion of them reflect the writers' anxiety about current problems. Among these latter are J. B. Priestley's 'Student Mobs', John Laycock's 'Guides to Dreamland', and Richard Church's 'Litter Bugs'. Young people usually believe that any adult discussion relating to themselves is slanted by jealousy or stuffiness. It is in fact more often directed—as here with Mr. Priestley and Mr. Laycock— to their elders' questioning of the behaviour of other elders: Is the mass hysteria of crowds of protesting students provoked by adult politicians thirsting for power? Is the mass hysteria surrounding pop groups stimulated by financiers hungry for profit from discs? What, anyway, are the ultimate individual and social consequences of mass hysteria? Is there a vital connection between mass hysteria and war? It is such questions as these that fill the two essays named with matter for debate, while Mr. Church's essay raises another question closely touching us all: Do we prefer to live in a clean country or in a filthy one?

There is matter for discussion on most pages of this book, but it has been compiled as much for enjoyment as for debate, though the two purposes are not necessarily separate. Sir Alan Herbert's imaginary legal case is an amusing approach to the question whether M.P.s should be paid and, if so, how much are their services to the country worth? And Mr. Jennings' comic piece on beards hits slily at advertisers' wiles, to which most of us are apt to succumb.

Among the rest, Sir Arthur Bryant the historian provides a vivid glimpse of the past, and Mr. Clarke (one of the best writers of science fiction) a brilliantly imaginative look into the future.

Not all the writers represented here are widely known or famous, for among the channels of communication now open to essayists, broadcasting has given opportunities to numerous authors who might not have found any opportunity through traditional literary channels. It is not only professional essayists who have something worthwhile to say. This book includes work by amateurs as well as professionals. Since no biographical information is available about several of the writers, it would have been invidious to give any about the better known. Students who require such information can find it at any public library if they consult the annual biographical reference book *Who's Who?*

Further words should be said about the contents of this anthology. Animals, birds, insects, trade, invention, children's games and picnics (with which 'Litter Bugs' are appropriately followed in the contents) all have a place. A concluding comment is needed on the Satire section. Satire is one of the most penetrating and powerful weapons ever devised against pretension, pomp and power in high places. But it is also a weapon that demands knowledge and skill from those who use it. It cannot be turned on to order in a hurry once a week, for satirists are rare; a Dryden or a Pope—to name two of the greatest English satirists—are not born every year. Those whose essays appear here under the Satire heading would not claim to be in the company of the greatest, but they have more than superficial knowledge of what they satirize, and they use their weapon with skill and without crude self-display. Mrs. Mortimer shrewdly chastises those who would huddle us all into a herd as a commercial or political convenience, instead of encouraging some measure of the separateness that allows for individuality and personal growth; Mr. Fitzgerald has stinging fun with one of the absurdities of present-day business habits, attacking from knowledge and with entertaining skill. Irony, a gentler though not less effective weapon than satire, gives point to the final sentence of *The Times* 'third Leader' on the use of our beaches. Though government and municipal officials are thought not to blush easily, this little essay should have caused some red faces in the right places and commanded that rare public (and private) virtue—commonsense.

WILLIAM GOLDING

Billy the Kid

ON THE first day, Lily, my nurse, took me to school. We went hand-in-hand through the churchyard, down the Town Hall steps, and along the south side of the High Street. The school was at the bottom of an alley; two rooms, one downstairs and one upstairs, a staircase, a place for hanging coats, and a lavatory. 'Miss' kept the school—handsome, good-tempered Miss, whom I liked so much. Miss used the lower room for prayers and sing-ing and drill and meetings, and the upper one for all the rest. Lily hung my coat up, took me upstairs and deposited me among a score or so of children who ranged in age from five to eleven. The boys were neatly dressed, and the girls over-dressed if anything. Miss taught in the old-fashioned way, catering for all ages at once.

I was difficult.

No one had suggested, before this time, that anything mattered outside myself. I was used to being adored, for I was an attractive child in an Anglo-Saxon sort of way. In-deed, my mother, in her rare moments of lyricism would declare that I had 'eyes like cornflowers and hair like a field of ripe corn'. I had known no one outside my own family—nothing but walks with Lily or my parents, and long holidays by a Cornish sea. I had read much for my age but saw no point in figures. I had a passion for words in themselves, and collected them like stamps or birds' eggs. I had also a clear picture of what school was to bring me. It was to bring me fights. I lacked opposition, and

B   I

yearned to be victorious. Achilles, Lancelot and Æneas should have given me a sense of human nobility but they gave me instead a desire to be a successful bruiser.

It did not occur to me that school might have discipline or that numbers might be necessary. While, therefore, I was supposed to be writing out my tables, or even dividing four oranges between two poor boys, I was more likely to be scrawling a list of words, butt (barrel), butter, butt (see goat). While I was supposed to be learning my Collect, I was likely to be chanting inside my head a list of delightful words which I had picked up God knows where—deebriss and Skirmishar, creskant and sweeside. On this first day, when Miss taxed me with my apparent inactivity, I smiled and said nothing, but nothing, until she went away.

At the end of the week she came to see my mother. I stuck my field of ripe corn round the dining-room door and listened to them as they came out of the drawing-room.

My mother was laughing gaily and talking in her front-door voice.

'He's just a little butterfly, you know—just a butterfly!'

Miss replied judiciously.

'We had better let that go for a while.'

So let go it was. I looked at books or pictures, and made up words, dongbulla for a carthorse; drew ships, and aeroplanes with all their strings, and waited for the bell.

I had quickly narrowed my interest in school to the quarter of an hour between eleven and fifteen minutes past. This was Break, when our society at last lived up to my expectations. While Miss sat at her desk and drank tea, we spent the Break playing and fighting in the space

between the desks and the door. The noise rose slowly in
shrillness and intensity, so that I could soon assess the
exact note at which Miss would ring a handbell and send
us back to our books. If we were dull and listless, Break
might be extended by as much as ten minutes; so there
was a constant conflict in my mind—a desire to be
rowdy, and a leader in rowdiness, together with the
knowledge that success would send us back to our desks.
The games were numerous and varied with our sex. The
girls played with dolls or at weddings. Most of the time
they played Postman's Knock among themselves—played
it seriously, like a kind of innocent apprenticeship.

Tap! Tap!
'Who's there?'
'A letter for Mary.'

We boys ignored them with a contempt of inexpres-
sible depth. We did not kiss each other, not we. We
played tag or fought in knots and clusters, while Miss
drank tea and smiled indulgently and watched our innocent apprenticeship.

Fighting proved to be just as delightful as I had
thought. I was chunky and zestful and enjoyed hurting
people. I exulted in victory, in the complete subjugation
of my adversary, and thought that they should enjoy it
too—or at least be glad to suffer for my sake. For this
reason, I was puzzled when the supply of opponents
diminished. Soon, I had to corner victims before I could
get a fight at all.

Imperceptibly the gay picture altered. Once back in
our desks, where the boys were safe from me, they
laughed at me, and sniggered. I became the tinder to a
catch word. Amazed, behind my eager fists, I watched
them and saw they were—but what were they? Appear-

ances must lie; for of course they could not drive themselves from behind those aimed eyes, could not persuade themselves that I, ego Billy, whom everyone loved and cherished, as by nature, could not persuade themselves that I was not uniquely woven of precious fabric—

Could it be?

Nonsense! Sky, fly, pie, soup, hoop, croup—geourgeous.

But there were whisperings in corners and on the stairs. There were cabals and meetings. There were conversations which ceased when I came near. Suddenly in Break, when I tried to fight, the opposition fled with screams of hysterical laughter, then combined in democratic strength and hurled itself on my back. As for the little girls, they no longer played Postman's Knock, but danced on the skirts of the scrum, and screamed encouragement to the just majority.

That Break ended early. When we were back at our desks, I found my rubber was gone, and no one would lend me another. But I needed a rubber, so I chewed up a piece of paper and used that. Miss detected my fault and cried out in mixed horror and amusement. Now the stigma of dirt was added to the others.

At the end of the morning I was left disconsolate in my desk. The other boys and girls clamoured out purposefully. I wandered after them, puzzled at a changing world. But they had not gone far. They were grouped on the cobbles of the alley, outside the door. The boys stood warily in a semi-circle, their satchels swinging loose like inconvenient shillelaghs. The girls were ranged behind them, ready to send their men into the firing line. The girls were excited and giggling, but the boys were pale and grim.

'Go on!' shouted the girls, 'go on!'

The boys took cautious steps forward.

Now I saw what was to happen—felt shame, and the bitterest of all my seven beings. Humiliation gave me strength. A rolled-up exercise book became an epic sword. I went mad. With what felt like a roar, but must really have been a pig-squeal, I leapt at the nearest boy and hit him squarely on the nose. Then I was round the semi-circle, hewing and thumping like Achilles in the river bed. The screams of the little girls went needle sharp. A second or two later, they and the boys were broken and running up the alley, piling through the narrow entry, erupting into the street.

I stood alone on the cobbles and a wave of passionate sorrow engulfed me. Indignation and affront, shame and frustration took command of my muscles and my lungs. My voice rose in a sustained howl, for all the world as though I had been the loser, and they had chased Achilles back to his tent. I began to zigzag up the alley, head back, my voice serenading a vast sorrow in the sky. My feet found their way along the High Street, and my sorrow went before me like a brass band. Past the Antique Shoppe, the International Stores, Barclay's Bank; past the tobacconist's and the Green Dragon, with head back, and grief as shrill and steady as a siren—

How can one record and not invent? Is there any point in understanding the nature of a small boy crying? Yet if I am to tell the small, the unimportant truth, it is a fact that my sorrows diminished unexpectedly and woefully up the street. What had been universal, became an army with banners, became soon so small that I could carry it before me, as it were, in two hands. Still indignant, still humiliated, still moving zigzag, with little running impulses and moments of pause, I had my grief

where I could hold it out and see it—look! Some complexity of nature added three persons to my seven devils
—or perhaps brought three of the seven to my notice.
There was Billy grieving, smitten to the heart; there was
Billy who felt the unfairness of having to get this grief all
the way home where his mother could inspect it; and
there was scientific Billy, who was rapidly acquiring
know-how.

I suspected that my reservoirs were not sufficient for
the waters of lamentation, suspected that my voice would
disappear, and that I was incapable of a half-mile's sustained emotion. I began to run, therefore, so that my
sorrow would last. When suspicion turned to certainty, I
cut my crying to a whimper and settled to the business of
getting it home. Past the Aylesbury Arms, across the
London Road, through Oxford Street by the Wesleyan
Chapel, turn left for the last climb in the Green—and
there my feelings inflated like a balloon, so that I did the
last twenty yards as tragically as I could have wished,
swimming through an ocean of sorrow, all, paradoxic-
ally enough, quite, quite genuine—swung on the front
door knob, stumbled in, staggered to my mother—

'Why, Billy! Whatever's the matter?'

—balloon bursts, floods, tempests, hurricanes, rage and
anguish—a monstrous yell—

'THEY DON'T LIKE ME!'

My mother administered consolation and the hesitant
suggestion that perhaps some of the transaction had been
my fault. But I was beyond the reach of such footling
ideas. She comforted, my father and Lily hovered, until
at last I was quiet enough to eat. My mother put on her
enormous hat and went out with an expression of grim
purpose. When she came back, she said she thought
everything would be all right. I continued to eat and

sniff and hiccup. I brooded righteously on what was going to happen to my school-fellows now that my mother had taken a hand. They were, I thought, probably being sent to bed without anything to eat, and it would serve them right and teach them to like me and not be cruel. After lunch, I enjoyed myself darkly (scaffole, birk, rake), inventing punishments for them—lovely punishments.

Miss called later and had a long talk with my mother in the drawing-room. As she left, I stuck my field of ripe corn round the dining-room door again and saw them.

'Bring him along a quarter of an hour late,' said Miss. 'That's all I shall need.'

My mother inclined her stately head.

'I know the children don't really mean any harm—but Billy is so sensitive.'

We were back to normal again, then. That night, I suffered my usual terrors; but the morning came and I forgot them again in the infinite promise of day. Lily took me to school a quarter of an hour later than usual. We went right in, right upstairs. Everyone was seated and you could have stuck a fork into the air of noiseless excitement. I sat in my desk, Lily went, and school began. Wherever I looked there were faces that smiled shyly at me. I inspected them for signs of damage but no one seemed to have suffered any crippling torment. I reached for a rubber, and a girl in pink and plaits leaned over.

A boy offered me a handkerchief. Another passed me a note with 'wil you jine my ggang' written on it. I was in. We began to say our tables and I only had to pause for breath before giving an answer to six sevens for a gale of whispers to suggest sums varying from thirty-nine to forty-five. Dear Miss had done her work well, and today

I should enjoy hearing her fifteen minutes' homily on brotherly love. Indeed, school seemed likely to come to a full stop from sheer excess of charity; so Miss, smiling remotely, said we would have an extra long break. My heart leapt, because I thought that now we could get on with some really fierce, friendly fighting, with even a bloodier nose. But Miss produced a train set. When the other boys got down to fixing rails, the girls, inexpressibly moved by the homily, seized me in posse. I never stood a chance against those excited arms, those tough, silken chests, those bird-whistling mouths, that mass of satin and serge and wool and pigtails and ribbons. Before I knew where I was, I found myself, my cornflowers popping out of my head, playing Postman's Knock.

The first girl to go outside set the pattern.

'A parcel for Billy Golding!'

In and out I went like a weaver's shuttle, pecked, pushed, hugged, mouthed and mauled, in and out from fair to dark to red, from Eunice who had had fever and a crop, to big Martha who could sit on her hair.

I kissed the lot.

This was, I suppose, my first lesson; and I cannot think it was successful. For I did not know about the homily, I merely felt that the boys and girls who tried to do democratic justice on me had been shown wrong. I was, and now they knew it, a thoroughly likeable character. I was unique and precious after all; and I still wondered what punishments their parents had found for them which had forced them to realize the truth.

I still refused to do my lessons, confronting Miss with an impenetrable placidity. I still enjoyed fighting if I was given the chance. I still had no suspicion that Billy was anything but perfect. At the end of term, when I went down to Cornwall, I sat in a crowded carriage with my prize book open on my knees for six hours (keroube, serrap, konfeederul), so that passengers could read the inscription. I am reading it now:

BILLY GOLDING
1919
PRIZE FOR
GENERAL IMPROVEMENT

NORMAN TURNER

The Month for Spo

ONE OF the great mysteries of the children's world—at least to an adult—is the way their games and customs swing into action year after year without any prompting. I used to think that astute shopkeepers kept special calendars as 'aides memoire'—March—marbles: April—skipping ropes: May—whips and tops: and so on. At the appropriate time they display the equipment in season and there you are.

This is all very improbable, of course, and yet the mystery remains in wait for a better answer. I was reminded of Spo one warm April day when my eldest child trotted home from school with a demand for it on her lips.

I had almost forgotten it. Away in the cobwebs of my mind were memories of summer days and long swigs of a cool liquid in a medicine bottle. That was Spo, a childhood drink that I hadn't noticed in the hands of a youngster for years. Yet here was a child of mine carrying on with a custom that has been practised in the northern hills for generations.

I've only come across Spo in the Pennines, and the southern Pennines at that. That is how I came to make it myself.

Most of my younger years were spent in an isolated village on the borders of Lancashire and Yorkshire. We hadn't much money to spare on such things as bottles of pop, and the cheapness of Spo was a blessing as well as a pleasure when summer days came round.

For a copper we could buy a lump of brittle liquorice at the chemists, shake it vigorously in a medicine bottle filled with water—it always was a medicine bottle—and we quickly had a tasty drink. When the bottle was empty, we simply refilled with water, shook it again, and there was another supply.

It was an old gentleman who lived near Rochdale in Lancashire who told me more about Spo. He died a year or two back when he was getting on for ninety but he remembered in his younger days walking up into the hills on Spo Sunday.

This was always the first Sunday in May. He told me of quite large parties of young people taking to the pack-horse trails on that day, even up to the 1890s, and making for Spo Pond.

I don't suppose that these Lancashire folk realized they were carrying on one of the spring traditions of centuries past when village people had their festivities to celebrate the passing of winter and the rebirth of the land. Mountain springs would be centres of such practices in the Pennines.

In some parts the name of this home-made drink is pronounced Spaw, and this gives a clue to its origin. It's a corruption of Spa, meaning a watering place as in Cheltenham or Harrogate Spa, and derived from the Belgian place of that name.

We can only guess when liquorice was first added to the spring water, or indeed why it was added at all! Maybe it gave a little 'body', or perhaps it hid the smell of some of the more obnoxious Spa waters?

My own feeling is that it was simply to disguise the taste of moorland waters. Anyone who has sampled water from the peat-covered hills will know that it is often unpalatable. Just as Moses sweetened the water in the wilderness by casting a tree into it, so our ancestors may have made their water pleasant by adding herbs.

A different trend took place in Derbyshire, where the water worship of the pagans developed into the well-known well dressings. Strangely though, there is a striking similarity between customs in the Peak District and those on the Lancashire/Yorkshire border. The children there drink water coloured with burnt sugar! This produces a drink of a like colour and taste to Spo.

My daughter knew nothing of all this. To her, Spo was a drink that she and her friends could make cheaply and with little trouble.

Perhaps it is not as popular as it once was in the towns. Bottles of pop have taken its place; but country children still enjoy a medicine bottle with its splodge of black in the bottom. And it has one claim that cannot be challenged. It was 'mineral water' long before our present-day orangeade and lime juice!

ANONYMOUS

Schoolboy Smokers

LOOKING BACK now I find it hard to remember when it began. I only know that one day, as I boarded a bus and noticed a thin mist of smoke curling between young heads bent over French and geographical textbooks I felt like the tourist who saw her first giraffe and exclaimed, 'I don't believe it.'

That some small boys smoked cigarettes, I had never doubted. That a number of schoolboys smoked regularly and heavily in the seclusion of the garden shed or amid dense woodland, I knew to be a fact. The habit had been deplored by the parents of my own generation which grew up in the 1930s. It had shocked the Victorians. Had not Dr. Gordon Stables, writing in 1896, declared: 'The boy who smokes grows up hen-hearted, nervous, easily led into vice, and if he does not die before he is thirty, but continues a slave to tobacco, he may be a monkey, but he isn't a man. . . . The remedy lies in the hand of the parent, and he must not spare the rod.'

Little Victorian boys did not smoke, surely, in the hansom-cab or the pony-cart that bore them home from school—or did they? Certainly, my own contemporaries of the 'thirties never dreamed of smoking in public. It was much too dangerous.

There we were in a crowded public bus travelling between green pastures and woodlands with names like Yokehurst and Oxebottom and Bineham that had not changed since Cornish and Flemish smugglers of the

13

sixteenth century first stepped ashore with the new
American weed called tobacco—and two young schoolboys were smoking.

That was ten years ago. The effect on their fellow
passengers was startling. Housewives fell silent, creased
their lips, watched the faint trails of smoke weaving to
and fro before the gay advertisements of a Brighton book-
maker. Husbands glared, and one was bold enough to
mutter, 'Look at those kids smoking.' Still more drama-
tic was the effect on fellow pupils of the two culprits—
and it was largely for this reason, I imagined, that the
pair indulged in the practice. The boys and girls around
them gazed at the smokers as though fascinated by the
strange spectacle.

It was then I regretted the absence of a Bus Passengers'
Charter. For what is one to do when an unknown youngster in a crowded bus breaks all the accepted rules of
schoolboy behaviour? I have seen strong men bend over
The Times crossword puzzle and pretend that they had
not noticed the youthful neighbour hurling inked pellets
of paper at the heads of fellow passengers, or producing
clouds of cigarette-smoke that drifted up the nostrils and
clouded the eyes.

Some people are braver and draw the conductor's attention to such matters. Is that wise? I have long admired
the courtesy and kindness of our south country bus conductors. I have also regretted that, faced with unruliness
among the young, they too often tend to fall into one or
other of two extremist groups. There are those who are
severe disciplinarians and those who are not. Those who
are may seek compensation for their own frustrations by
making much of very little. A young offender, and probably his innocent companions as well, may find themselves banished from the bus and left to walk the four

or five miles to home or school. Conductors falling into the second category may be skittish and facetious—and swiftly transform the faintly obstreperous into the rowdy.

What can a passenger do? He can adopt the role of the kindly uncle—'Now look here, old man . . .'—and risk being rewarded with cheek. He may try the art of persuasion, with a note of authority in the voice as he says, 'Look—must you do that?' As a rule this method works, for the majority of schoolboys today, to judge from my own experience in a pleasant corner of rural England, are better behaved and more amenable to reason than my own generation ever were. When they are not, and it is clear that a school's reputation is suffering, a word to their headmaster may be the only remedy. But it must be a tactful word. Failing that, the passenger can only take the law into his own hands and utter what I can best describe as a secondary modern snarl.

I have recently adopted this course on two occasions. Each time the results astonished me. Paper pellets were quickly restored to pockets, cigarettes were extinguished, and boys who seemed bent on doing each other severe bodily harm relaxed into an uneasy calm.

Such a weapon cannot be used every day. It must be reserved for special occasions. An offence like smoking by schoolboys—and schoolgirls—in buses and trains is an all too common occurrence. This is no exaggeration. Recently, finding myself stranded on the outskirts of our market town, I caught the four o'clock bus and found I was stepping out of the clear downland air into an atmosphere heavily clouded with the smoke from a dozen cigarettes. All the smokers were boys and they wore the uniforms of four different schools. 'My doctor does want me to cut it down,' admitted a most courteous lad of about sixteen, who sat himself beside me. He spoke of boys being given cigarettes as a birthday present from their parents.

'What does your headmaster think about it?' I inquired.

'The only time we discussed it he was at the other end of a cane,' replied the boy.

The bus halted and two more schoolboys clambered aboard. One carried a cigarette prominently displayed behind his left ear, as if for show. The other child promptly produced a small packet of cigarettes and a box of matches from inside his shirt. He did not look more than about eleven years of age.

The first boy suddenly caught my eye and the cigarette vanished. We happen to be neighbours.

'What would your parents say if they knew?' I demanded, later that evening. 'They do know, sir. Dad says you are quite right to object to boys smoking in the buses. He says that if I want a smoke I should go behind a hedge.'

We talked for twenty minutes about the increasing popularity of smoking among schoolboys, and the cost to the health and the pocket. 'I don't smoke much, sir,' said this twelve-year-old.

His companion insisted that there were times when one simply had to smoke or be considered 'green'. He never bought cigarettes. They were always given to him by other boys or by grown-ups. He began smoking at the age of eleven, when travelling by train to his private school. 'You must admit, sir, that there's an awful lot of it, with folks having so much money to burn.'

I ventured to explain why I was a non-smoker. 'Please, sir, when did you stop smoking?'

'When I was twelve,' I answered, truthfully.

JOHN LAYCOCK

Guides to Dreamland

THIS WEEK's public offer of shares in the Beatles, and the
emergence of John Lennon as a company director, are
only the latest reminder of the profits to be picked up out
of 'pop'.

Over the last two years, some twenty-five new 'pop'
magazines have appeared. From general monthlies and
weeklies with pictures and news of the 'pop' world
(*Rave, Big Beat, Fabulous*), through monthly fan-club
publications (*Beatles Book*), to various weekly newspapers (some, like *Combo*, new; others, like *New Musical
Express* and *Melody Maker*, adapted to the 'pop' world),
they all aim to guide the teenage world along easily ex-
ploitable lines. They cost from 6d. for a 12-page newspaper (*Combo*), to 2s. 6d. for a 64-page 'glossy' (*Rave*),
and come mainly from three publishing organizations.

Exact circulation figures are hard to come by. *Rave,
Big Beat, Fabulous, Beatles Book* all exceed 150,000; and
New Musical Express is as high as 300,000. Many of the
others fall not far short of this, although a few—like *Billy
Fury Monthly*—sell no more than 35,000.

'Pop' magazines provide teenagers with a dreamland
and, in so doing, exploit commercially the teenagers'
problems and insecurities. To tell their readers what is
'with it' they adopt—and sometimes create—the 'with it'
language of the teenage world. Vocabulary is limited and
highly stereotyped; adjectives are usually 'fab', 'gear',
'fun', 'in', 'big', 'crisp', 'dreamy', 'swinging'. No dis-

crimination is shown between conventional parts of speech: 'to wax a demonstration disc which will show-case their talents' is standard procedure. Some of the language is simply illiterate: 'I still think he could happen very very big in this country.' And nearly all of it is monotonous.

After using 'with it' language, the magazines proceed to set the right materialistic atmosphere for exploitation; 'The Mojos were off on a shopping expedition . . . they shared out £500—and that's not peanuts!' But money is no end in itself: 'Of course, money gives you the power to buy things and do things that were just in the imagination before.'

Accordingly, exact details of what every teenager should buy are provided—first, by describing what the stars are buying: 'Mick's gone mad on round thin-neck sweaters. Brian raves over a 30 gn. French jacket he bought at Cecil Gee's . . . recently he spent £12 buying eight shirts'; secondly, by editorial pontificating on what is 'in': 'Rouge is big right now. . . . Use rouge on your kneecaps in cold weather. It gets rid of those romance-killing blue patches.'

Sex in 'pop' magazines is only hinted at. Male stars stand in effeminately suggestive positions, and adolescent emotions are fastened to externals like hair (of great sexual significance). Thus, *Big Beat* suggests that one star's success is due to 'the long hair tied back with the Tom Jones bow', and girls appeal for boy friends who 'must have long hair'. Only scant references are made to the boy or girl you should admire: 'We don't really go for the mousy, girl-next-door type. We like girls who are interesting and trend-setting. A girl with lots of personality and exciting, exotic hobbies.'

Boys are mainly 'fab' or 'dreamy' or just 'good looking,

especially when his face is tanned by stage make-up'. Always the same meaningless terms are used: Mick Jagger, writes one reader, 'just oozes with sex, excitement, and sparkle'.

Sex is only hinted at because it is real—it belongs to the everyday world and its problems. Bring it openly into 'pop' magazines, and you bring responsibilities that will shatter dreamland and end the sense of security dreamland induces. *Big Beat* can indeed assert, 'When you think about it, "pop" is the most romantic thing. A boy sings a song about love—and the girls love him and the song. . . . We even believe the words they put to the tunes!' This is make-believe, nothing to do with real sexual relationships. Beatles may marry, but in the magazines we only hear of marriage as part of this dreamland; *Rave* asks, 'Could you marry a Stone?' and gives a marriage-consultant's advice on the ideal wives for the Rolling Stones.

'Pop' magazines reflect few permanent values. The only thing that really matters is not to be a square or a 'Fuddyduddy': 'The Beatles would hate to appear corny.' To a great extent, of course, this is a rejection of dull middleclass conformity: 'What we need are more alive and interesting faces.' The sad thing is that 'interesting' means nothing more positive than 'different'; so in the end they have to clutch at the only reality they can find in dreamland, the only thing that is inescapably theirs alone: youth. 'We're young. Youth is on our side. And it's youth that matters right now.'

But it's not really any comfort, for youth is a transitory value that vanishes as they watch: 'The thing I'm afraid of is growing old. I hate that. You get old and you've missed it somehow.' (John Lennon.) And this pitiful fear of growing old, of missing 'it' (whatever 'it' may be), is the fear of having to leave the magic dreamland; but it has great commercial possibilities.

The actual building up of dreamland is an easy task. The reader is assured that the stars are really all ordinary lads, so that he can identify himself with them and the magic dreamland of their life. Just like you, Reader, says *Big Beat*, The Animals 'are not really far removed from those five boys who once had to toss up as to who should sleep on the camp bed and who on the floor in the bare room they all once shared'. But the reporter is essential in forming a stepping-stone between reality and dreamland. *Rave's* reporter Cathy confides: 'I think you're going to have a great time sharing my life with the stars. . . . I come from an average home. In most ways I am the same as the next girl. What has happened to me could just as well have happened to you.' Finally, the reader's involvement is clinched by telling him of the power he has over the stars: 'You set the scene, call the tune, make or break the stars.'

Values of the real world are ignored or scorned: 'In case you hadn't noticed,' jeers *Fabulous*, 'they're having a general election. Most of us aren't old enough to vote in it. Who cares!' A fan who writes to *The Rolling Stones Book* says she is 'lost in time, suspended from reality'. 'Pop' magazines know how to keep her there.

SIR ARTHUR BRYANT

A Holiday in Time

I WANT you to imagine yourself about to take a journey[1] from a little town somewhere in the northern Midlands to London, not today but two hundred and fifty years ago, that is in the reign of James II. It is a town in a remote, hilly district, a day's journey from the great main road which links London to the north and where the new-fashioned stagecoaches run. Like most of your neighbours and indeed most Englishmen of the time, you have never been to London or anywhere farther than a day's ride to the nearest Assize town, where you once went when you had a small law-suit about a field. But this is to be a much greater journey on very important business—nothing else could justify the time and expense of such an undertaking—and you have been putting it off all the winter till the rains stopped and the floods subsided and the roads dried a little after their annual drenching.

Of course, though you are going to business, it is all rather an adventure. You have never done such a journey before and in the course of your life you are never likely to again. So though you rather dread the dangers and discomforts, you are rather thrilled. For a long time past you have been making preparations, buying clothes for the journey and discussing with your neighbours the

[1] Originally broadcast under the title *Travelling in James II's England*.

best way of reaching London. After thinking it over you
have decided to ride to the nearest posting town on the
great north road, where you have booked a place in one
of the new-fashioned flying-coaches that ply from York to
London during the summer in the almost incredibly short
space of four days—that is, as the advertisement in the
town coffee-house is careful to point out, 'if God permit.'
There are only three of them a week, so you were careful to book your seat a month or so before, and have paid
thirty-five shillings for it with an extra ten shillings
premium for the advance booking. It seems a lot of
money, when you remember that that sum is equivalent
to at least nine or ten times as much as it would be today, but, short of being a gentleman with a private coach
of your own or a Crœsus who can afford to hire a post-
chaise, it is the most comfortable and rapid means of
travel available—and, as you are never likely to have the
chance of doing the journey again, it seems well worth it.

Well, the great day arrives. Very early, before it is
light—for, with the vast distances you have to cover, every
hour of daylight is precious—you get up and dress by
candlelight in the travelling clothes you have bought or
borrowed for the occasion—high boots thickly beeswaxed,
a thick leather riding-suit and a long cloak coming down
to your spurs to keep off the dust and mud. And, knowing there may be footpads or highwaymen, you are careful to add a pair of pistols and a sword—the one your
father wore at the battle of Edgehill. Then, clanking a
little ponderously over the cobble stones and waking up
some of your neighbours as you go, you make your way
down the dark familiar streets to the George Inn, where
for the sum of 3d. a mile for the sixty miles or so you
have to cover you have hired a horse from your friend
the host, who being also the local postmaster always keeps

three or four post-horses for travellers. The ostler is waiting with it in the courtyard beside the mounting-stone, so
you hastily swallow your morning draught of mulled ale
and pull yourself into the saddle. A guide from the inn,
who is to accompany you as far as the coaching town, is
waiting also with a led horse on which your luggage is
slung.

A minute later you are trotting over the cobble stones
and out into the country with the guide and the led
horse beside you. In front, winding over hill and dale,
stretches your road. It is not a smooth white metalled
road with clearly defined sides like a modern road, but
a soft grassy trackway, marked by horse hoofs and ruts.
Near the town the ruts have been ploughed up by the
parish-plough which is taken from its home under the
church porch every spring for this purpose. But soon these
signs of civilization vanish, and the winter's ruts, often
five or six feet deep, are untouched, with only an occasional sprinkling of stones or faggots thrown down in
the worst places. You soon slacken pace and subside into
a walk. In the muddier parts you find it better to leave
the highway and ride beside it in the fields. The road
seems to have gone native: sometimes a broad grassy
trackway with the hedges and bushes cut back twenty
yards or more on either side, as the regulations against
robbers require, and at others only a narrow lane between
high hedges and so narrow in places that you have to
ride in single file to avoid being scratched by the
brambles. Presently it becomes hilly and the track full of
large smooth pebbles which make the horses slip, so that
you are forced every now and then to dismount and lead
them. And at the bottom of every valley there is a stream
and a ford through which you splash. There are no
bridges in this district, except for a few quaking, shak-

ing structures of neglected stone or wood, full of holes and so narrow that you can scarcely persuade your horse to cross. It is a lonely part of the world, and you meet few people on the road, mostly farmers and peasants going about their business. Their produce, you notice, is carried on wooden frames loaded high and corded on the horses' backs instead of being slung on either side in the usual panniers. This is because of the narrowness of the lanes, your guide tells you.

On the crests of the hills you can see the country spread before you—far wilder than the England of today—a rolling plain with few hedges or fences, and here and there dark with great woods and forests. Much of it is waste and heath: only round the villages, where you stop for a few minutes for refreshment at a smoking ale-house hung with spiders' webs, are there ploughed fields, and these without hedges and cut up into innumerable strips like vast allotments. Between the villages there is little sign of cultivation, save for a few scraggy cattle and tiny sheep, and occasionally some geese and swine, with here and there a wretched hovel of sticks and straw where the smoke of some poor squatters rises into the early summer air. But the sun is shining and the birds are singing, and it all looks good to you.

So you ride all day, till your seat grows sore beneath you and begin to wish you had spent a few more days in the winter accustoming yourself to horseback. Your boots are splashed high with mud and your cloak and saddle-cloth thick with dust. Once you lose your way, for there are so many tracks branching out to left and right that even the guide is often puzzled. Fortunately a friendly pedlar, sleeping by the roadside after selling his wares at some lonely hamlet, sets you on your way again. Only once do you see a signpost—the very first in these parts, your companion tells you—and your best guides are the church spires and belfries of the villages along the way. Once, as you reach the top of a hill, there is a more ominous landmark: a tall gibbet and on it, creaking and swaying in the wind, a fading corpse with a few poor shreds of clothing hanging from it, and a cluster of ugly kites hovering overhead. The guide tells you, with a grim laugh, that the corpse was once a highwayman, who has been hung to discourage others on the spot where once he committed his robberies.

A little before it begins to get dark you descend a long winding hill and start to cross a great plain. Presently the road turns into a narrow causeway, paved with rough stones, and on either side a dark marsh from which an evil-smelling white mist is beginning to rise and the sound of strange birds calling out eerily! It reminds you of the narrow road across the Valley of the Shadow of Death of which you have been reading in Mr. Bunyan's, the non-conformist preacher's book, the *Pilgrim's Progress*. Suddenly there is the sound of a jingling bell, and then eyes shine before you in the gathering darkness and shadowy forms loom up on the causeway. A man calls out angrily, and you feel for your pistols. But a moment later you are reassured, for it is only a train of pack-horses carrying ironware towards the town from which you have come. Still, it is inconvenient enough for, being only two to their fifty, you and your guide have to clamber down the slippery side of the causeway into the mud below while the long procession of laden horses winds by like an infinitely slow luggage-train, the warning bell jingling on the leading horse and the pack-horse men swearing and cursing out of the darkness.

Wearily, and muddy now up to the saddle-girths, you lead your horse back on to the causeway and remount.

Soon it is quite dark. You are hungry and cold and fear that the fenny mist around you will breed an ague and ache in every limb of your body. Then, far away, you hear the sound of church bells and see faint lights, and the guide tells you that your journey is almost done. It is past eight o'clock and you have been in the saddle with a few brief halts since five. But you have ridden the sixty miles you had to travel—in winter you could not have done half the distance—and here before you is the posting town on the Great North Road. A few minutes later your horse, pricking up his ears, canters into the courtyard of the chief inn of the place—the station from which the London coach starts in the morning. It has already arrived and disgorged its passengers, and you can see its great shadowy form in the darkness.

A servant comes running out with a lantern, an ostler takes your horse, and a moment later you are being escorted up a broad oak staircase to a room where, since you are resolved to spare no expense and have the best of everything, a fire is quickly lit and a cup of sack brought you by mine host himself. With a bow he asks you whether you will have your supper served in your chamber or dine with your fellow travellers of the morrow in the ordinary downstairs. You elect the latter. After a servant has pulled off your great boots and taken off your heavy cloak and sword, you go downstairs and join the company in a smoke-filled room before a mighty fire. Here you eat heartily, drink deep of the innkeeper's incomparable strong waters, and fall asleep to an accompaniment of mine host's broad jokes and long stories about jackises and horse-races. At last you stagger up to bed and are soon snoring loudly, unwoken even by the fleas and the croaking of the frogs under the floor, which are the hostlery's only defect—for it is a capital house and one of England's most famous inns.

You are roused early in the morning—just before it is light—and to music. For there in the narrow street below your window is the town band come to give you and your fellow travellers a *levite*—a favour for which, though unasked, you have to vail or tip them, as you also have to the ostler, the servants and your guide of yesterday. Then you swallow your morning draft—a bottle of Northdown ale and some pickled oysters—and proceed to take your place in the coach. It is a formidable-looking vehicle with a domed roof and a square body covered with black leather and studded with brass nails, and swung on leather straps suspended from tall axle-trees. In front sits the coachman with a vast red cloak and wide laced sleeves, and in front of him six great black shire horses pawing the stones impatiently. The luggage is strapped on to a platform on the back, and, after a scramble for the best seat in which you are a little too slow for your more experienced fellow travellers, you take your seat, a gentleman of leisure, in the boot of the coach.

It is a fine day, so you and your fellow passengers open the leather flap that serves for window and look out at the sights of the road. They are worth seeing, for this is the greatest road in the country, and half England seems afoot or a-horse. The road is much broader than the one you travelled yesterday, though still only a soft, ill-defined trackway of grass and trampled earth, for the raised and metalled Roman road which ran here vanished centuries ago. All over it horsemen and pedestrians, herds of cattle and livestock and country carts drawn by oxen and horses are winding and zig-zagging to avoid the holes and the enormous ruts into which it has been cut by the winter traffic. The coach creaks, sways, rolls and plunges—it is travelling at a smart pace of five miles an hour, unthinkable till a few years back for wheeled traffic—and a young gentleman in the corner complains that he feels sick and wishes that he had taken the advice of his old father, the Yorkshire squire, and ridden to London in the good old-fashioned way. Still, it is something to feel that you are travelling in one of the fastest vehicles on one of the fastest roads in the world: there is a good deal to be said for progress after all. It is better than crawling along in a stage-wagon, with thirty other passengers of all classes crowded together on the wooden floor under the arched cloth hood and covering a bare twelve or fifteen miles a day: it would take a fortnight to reach London that way. Just at that moment you start to pass one—a vast, long covered wagon with eight horses one behind the other, with plumes and bells, and the wagoner with a long whip walking beside. He and the guard of your coach exchange such a volley of broad country oaths and jests that the lady opposite you blushes crimson.

The sights of the road are never ending; country carts and laden farm horses, pedlars and chapmen with their packs and trays, pedestrians with bundles on their backs and red-faced Justices with their grinning servants riding to their business; a travelling merchant with three or four led horses carrying samples of cloth, and every now and then a gentlewoman riding pillion behind husband or groom. Once or twice in the hour you pass a gentleman's coach, emblazoned with heraldry, the six fine horses drawing it shaking their brightly coloured reins and a footman in livery going before to open the gates and remove boulders and other obstacles from the road. About midday, just before you draw up at the inn of a tiny market town to dine, you see a royal courier riding past with His Majesty's arms and mails. All the while the country folk are passing and repassing, going to market or driving their flocks, while in the great fields beside the open road haymakers and shepherds are attending to their business.

Every few miles the coach splashes through the ford of some stream, while tiny runlets and water-courses cross the road almost constantly. Once there is a halt of several minutes while the coach waits its turn at a narrow stone bridge over a broad river. All this, though the sun is shining brightly, keeps the coach well plastered with mud, and at least twice you are forced to alight while a score or so of country labourers shoulder it out of a deep rut into which it has fallen and almost overturned. It is obvious that all this wheeled traffic, which has recently superseded the purely foot and horse travelling of earlier days, is playing havoc with the English road system: it is no longer any use doing, as the old statute that governed highway maintenance laid down, leaving the roads alone that they 'may grow better of themselves'. With so many wheels, wind and sun are not enough, and even the new Acts of Parliament, which restrict the number of draught-horses and insist on a regulation thickness of wheel-rims, seems to do little good. Frequently in the neighbourhood of villages you pass gangs of labourers, cutting away overgrowing brambles from the sides of the highway and shovelling loose earth into the worst holes. But they work lazily enough, for the law, which enforces on each parishioner six days a year statute-labour on the parish highways, is only loosely observed, and statute-labour is regarded more as a holiday and a means of begging alms from travellers than anything else. Over and over again the coach is surrounded by a swarm of such labourers, the King's Highwaymen, as they are called; one of your fellow travellers suggests that the King's Loiterers would be a better name.

So your journey continues. Occasionally the coach shakes and jolts, rumbling like a cannon, over the cobbles of some narrow-streeted, evil-smelling town, but such are few and far between. Once on a lonely stretch of road one of the axle-trees breaks, and you have to wait some hours till it is mended. The last time he travelled to London, a lawyer in the company tells you, the coach overturned twice so that all his fellow passengers fell on top of him and strained the joints of his leg, while on another occasion the traces broke and the horses went on, leaving them all sitting in the middle of the road.

The worst part of the journey is on the third day when you travel through the region of heavy midland clay, where the road between Biggleswade and Baldock is so bad that the coach is forced to break through a hedge and take to the fields to avoid the slough of despond between the hedges. The country folk hereabouts are busy collecting tolls from travellers who are driven to this course. All this takes so long that the coach does not reach the inn at Baldock till almost midnight, and it is too late to get supper.

All through the fourth and last day of your journey the sights of habitation and the concourse of travellers increase. Everything seems to be converging on the metropolis. Every half-mile or so, a cloud of dust proclaims a drove of cattle, hogs, sheep or geese, winding in a long column towards the London slaughter-house which is the lodestar of their poor lives. Here the roads are a veritable quagmire, sodden with the ordure of this never-ceasing procession of doomed beasts, and you are forced to stop your nose to avoid the smell.

For the last hour or two of the afternoon the scene again changes, and you cross a desolate lonely upland with scarcely a house in sight. The guard loads his pistols and you peer anxiously at the clumps of bushes. For here on wild Finchley Heath is the most perilous stage of all your journey—the haunt of the London highwaymen. Here every fellow traveller is an object of suspicion, and a group of cloaked horsemen coming up over the brow of a hill just ahead causes a regular panic. But it turns out to be a troop of dragoons who are on the lookout for a gang who robbed a great Lord's coach only this morning, a few hundred yards from this very spot.

Just before sunset you turn a little out of the main stream of traffic and climb the long ascent to Highgate. Here, across a belt of two more miles of green fields, you can see the towers and spires of London, now rising again after the great fire of twenty years before, and far off by the river a forest of masts. Then, as it grows dark, the streets close about you and the hoofs and wheels rattle on the cobbles. To your country ears the noise is like the roaring of the sea: endless faces peer into the coach and the rich smell of crowded humanity assails your nostrils. Tired and bewildered as you are, it is all immensely exciting. All of a sudden there is a tremendous scraping and groaning and the coach is stuck fast in a narrow street between the stone posts on either side. It is too dark by now to extricate it, and, stiff and dazed, you clamber out. There is nothing for it but to leave your luggage with the guard till morning and walk to your inn. A crowd of beggars, clutching and mumbling, surrounds you, a ragged link-boy appears with a flaming torch to escort you, and, with your fellow travellers and a bundle of hastily gathered belongings, you set out through the London lanes and alleys to finish your journey on Shanks's pony.

ARTHUR C. CLARKE

Seas of Tomorrow

THE SEA covers two-thirds of the planet we have mis-
named Earth, and is so much a part of our lives, our
traditions and our culture that we think of it as something universal, eternal. Yet it is neither; it is unique to
our world, and all its sagas may be no more than one
other chapter of history.

For in the beginning, there was no sea. The burning
rocks of the newly formed Earth were too hot for water
to condense upon them. Without a break, century after
century, the greatest storms our planet has ever known
raged from pole to pole, but the rain boiled skyward into
steam when it touched the ground. The whole world was
dry land.

And one day, the geologists and the Book of Revelation
agree, it will be dry again. As our planet ages, it will
slowly lose its envelope of air and water. The atmosphere will drift off into space; the oceans will sink
down through cracks and crevices as the face of the
once beautiful Earth wrinkles like that of an old, old
woman.

Seas and lakes and rivers belong to the morning glory
of a world, and do not long outlast its youth. We know
that this is true, for there is an analogy close at hand.
When we look outward from the Sun, we see a world
that has already lost its oceans, for only a trace of water
remains upon our neighbour Mars, locked up at the
poles in a thin powdering of snow. And if—which seems

unlikely—the Moon ever possessed oceans, it, too sur-
rendered them long ago to space.

At this moment of time, it appears, no other world
knows the march of waves against the shore, the ebb and
flow of tides, the white line of foam retreating down the
beach. These things belong to Earth alone; the inner
planets are too hot for water to exist upon them in liquid
form, the outer ones, far too cold.

There is only one possible exception, and even that is
not very promising. This is the planet Venus, almost a
twin of the Earth in size, but some twenty-five million
miles nearer to the Sun.

Venus, now the target for an increasing number of
space probes and radar beams, is covered with perpetual
clouds, which through the telescope appear as a blind-
ing, featureless white. The spectroscope shows that there
is water on Venus, but it may all be in the clouds, for
recent radio measurements indicate that the surface
temperature of the planet is far above boiling point. However, these figures are not yet final; it is still possible that
Venus has seas, or at least lakes, in her polar regions or
at high mountain altitudes.[1] There may even be tempor-
ary seas that condense on the dark side of the planet as
it slowly rotates; we shall soon know.

Yet when we think of the word 'sea', we may be taking too parochial a view. Need an ocean be made of
water? There are other possibilities, and in the enormous, multiform complexity of the universe, many of them
may be realized. On the giant worlds, Jupiter and Saturn,
circling in the outer cold far beyond the orbit of Mars,

---

[1] Even the Mariner readings, which appeared to confirm the high
temperature, have been disputed by some scientists. Venus seems
determined to keep her secrets to the end.

D

there may be—indeed, we can almost say there *are*—
oceans greater than any upon our own planet.

These oceans, if we can call them that, are hundreds
of miles deep, and formed of liquid ammonia. They are
stirred by storms so tremendous that we can see them
across more than a billion miles of space. And drifting
sluggishly across the southern hemisphere of Jupiter is a
strange floating island as large as our entire Earth, the
famous Red Spot, perhaps the only permanent feature of
the planet's ever-changing surface. For Jupiter is a world
without geography.

It seems unlikely that men will ever explore the turbu-
lent, icy depths of these strange seas. But before many
years have passed, our robot space probes will be descend-
ing through the atmospheres of the giant planets, brav-
ing the ammonia storms to radio information back to
distant Earth.

What will they find there? Today, we do not know
enough even to make intelligent guesses. Every astrono-
mer will assure you that no form of life could possibly
exist on Jupiter or Saturn, at temperatures of two or
three hundred degrees below zero, and pressures of a
thousand tons to the square inch. But it is worth remembering that only a century ago the biologists were equally
certain that no life could exist in the depths of our own
oceans.

There may even be 'seas' on the Moon; if there are, they
will be of dust. Some astronomers have suggested that the
flat lunar plains may be covered with finely divided pow-
der that has been flaked from the mountains by the relent-
less blasts of solar radiation. Dry and slippery as talcum,
it could have gathered during the ages in low-lying
areas, where it may be waiting to trap future
explorers.

As I have suggested in a novel *A Fall of Moondust*, it could be very unpleasant stuff to negotiate. In some ways it would behave just like a normal liquid, flowing slowly under the low lunar gravity. You could walk across it with the aid of skis or snow shoes, and one day there may be paddle-wheel moon boats sailing the lunar seas, long after they are extinct on Earth. This delightfully nostalgic idea was first suggested by the science-fiction writer James Blish, and I hope that one day he receives due credit. It will also be an amusing irony if the old astronomers who gave the Latin names *Mare* and *Oceanus* to many of the dark plains on the Moon turn out to have been not so far off the mark after all.

Much more formidable seas may exist on some parts of Mercury, the nearest planet to the Sun. It is hot enough here to melt sulphur, and possibly even such metals as lead and tin. There may be regions of the planet where the temperature never falls much below a thousand degrees Fahrenheit, for Mercury keeps one face turned always towards the Sun.

Above any valleys on the day side of Mercury, the Sun could hang almost vertically overhead forever, while its rays—ten times as powerful as on Earth—reverberated from the surrounding walls. From such valleys might flow rivers of molten metal, seeking, as do the rivers of Earth, their own infernal seas. Any mariners who ever brave these fiery oceans will require stout ships indeed.

But even molten metal is something that we can understand and can handle with techniques which date back five thousand years or more. However, at the very frontier of the solar system, almost four billion miles from the Sun, we may encounter the strangest and perhaps most terrible seas of all.

On the outermost planet Pluto, the noon temperature

may occasionally soar to 350 degrees *below* zero. On the dark side, it must be much colder; the aptly named Plutonian night lasts six times as long as ours, and in the small hours of the morning it may grow cold enough to liquefy hydrogen.

We are now handling liquid hydrogen on the large scale as a rocket fuel, and it is most peculiar stuff. Quite apart from its extreme coldness—it boils if allowed to become warmer than minus 423°F.—it is extraordinarily light, having less than a tenth of the density of water. Any vessel of normal design would thus sink like a log in a sea of hydrogen; even balsa wood or cork would plummet to the bottom like lead.

Whether or not there are hydrogen lakes on Pluto is, today, anyone's guess, and it will be quite a while before we know the answer. But there is one yet stranger possibility that should be mentioned; if Pluto cannot provide it, it must surely occur somewhere in the cosmos, perhaps on a giant Jupiter-like planet that has lost its sun and been frozen for ages in the interstellar night.

The ultimate ocean—the sea to end all seas—is one of liquid helium. At the unimaginable temperatures of minus 455°F.—only four degrees above the absolute zero of temperature—helium turns into a fluid called Helium II. This is a substance absolutely unique in the universe, with properties that defy common sense and even logic.

This is what could happen, if the explorers of the far future ever meet a sea of Helium II and are reckless enough to set sail upon it. To get a better picture of the improbable events that would follow, we will assume that our mariners are using an open boat.

They would get their first surprise immediately after they pushed off from the shore. Whereas on water—or any other liquid—friction brings a moving body to rest within seconds, this does not happen with Helium II. It is almost completely frictionless; by comparison, the smoothest ice is like sandpaper. The boat would therefore head out to sea with undiminished velocity, without benefit of motor. It would eventually reach the far shore —even if that were a thousand miles away—if something much more disconcerting did not happen first.

The voyagers would suddenly become aware that their boat was filling at an alarming rate. We can assume, of course, that they have already checked it carefully for leaks, and are confident that none exist. Then why is Helium II rising so rapidly above the floorboards?

Though the boat has plenty of freeboard, the stuff is coming *straight up the side and over the gunwales*, in a thin but swiftly moving film that is defying gravity. For Helium II can syphon itself from one container into another, provided that there is a connecting path between the two. In this case, the process will stop only when the level inside the boat is the same as that outside; and by then, of course, it will have sunk. . . .

Let us suppose that our explorers, a little shaken, manage to get back to land and build themselves a better boat. Obviously, it must be totally enclosed, not an open dinghy, but something like a submarine. They check the hull very carefully for leaks, going over every inch of it with a magnifying glass. Not even a pinhole is visible, so they set sail again with complete confidence.

All that happens this time is that their ship takes a little longer to sink. Helium II is a 'superfluid' that can race like lightning through microscopic pores and holes. Even a hull that was, for all practical purposes, airtight, would leak like a sieve in a sea of Helium II.

After these imaginary, yet possible, adventures, it is a relief to return to the familiar seas of Earth. We will never escape their call, as long as we are human. For we were born in water, and the salts of the ancient oceans still flow through our veins, though we left them half a billion years ago.

Whatever strange oceans the men of the future find upon far worlds, they will never love them as we loved the seas of Earth.

BERNARD DARWIN

The Spirit of Picnic

THE ESSENTIAL quality of a picnic is the doing of perfectly normal things in an abnormal place or manner. Those who prefer the beaten track of meals, the seedy, commonplace round of every day, will never be happy at a picnic. A famous Cambridge character of bygone days, on being bidden by an eager hostess to some such enterprise, replied in the single, devastating sentence, 'But the bread and butter will be so smeary.' Persons having souls so dead will never enjoy lunch out of a paper bag in a third, or even a first-class railway carriage. But to those of a more youthful spirit there is something positively holy about a hard-boiled egg eaten in such circumstances. Nobody wishes to devour hard-boiled eggs forever, nor to have the salt wrapped up in a screw of newspaper. Neither in ordinary life do we live for choice on sandwiches, which if eaten rapidly one after the other, as they invariably are, produce a curious sensation of breathlessness. Yet on a journey they are infinitely exciting, and it was one of the few good things about war-time travel, when restaurant cars either ceased to be or were unattainable through the solid mob in the corridor, that sandwiches came into their own again. They could no longer be made of ham, and it is, to me at any rate, one of the unsolved mysteries of life that whereas cold beef is among the most divine of foods, cold beef sandwiches are among the least appetising. Still the old childish joy was there.

There were other circumstances in war-time far less

attractive in which something of that ancient sensation could be recaptured. During the Battle of Britain a good many of us spent broken, 'noisy' nights in the cellar, trying to sleep uneasily in easy chairs and periodically declaring that the latest crash came from several miles further off than it palpably did. Nothing could be more odious and yet when at some uncharted hour of the night cocoa was made and biscuits handed round there was more in them than mere comfort. There was romance, the ineffable romance of a picnic underground. Not far from my home are the famous Chislehurst caves, where during the war so many people spent their nights that for several months a special train ran every night from Cannon Street to take them there. That they were originally driven to this city of refuge by romantic motives I would not go so far as to say, but that the children at least must have derived an unfading delight from their surroundings I cannot doubt, especially if they were told the pleasing legend that the caves had been made with the antlers of deer by the Druids. At any rate, I like to think that some day they will say to one another with a great thrill of speech, 'Do you remember what fun it was having our supper in Chislehurst Caves?'

It cannot, I suppose, be denied that a love of picnics is not an irrefutable evidence of character, that sometimes the very best of people do not like picnics and the very worst do. There is a passage in *Emma* which always makes me rather uncomfortable. There is to be a party to pick strawberries at Donwell, and Mrs. Elton, after descanting on the bonnet she will wear and the basket she will carry, the one with the pink ribbons, declares that it is to be 'a sort of gipsy party—a table spread in the shade, you know. Everything as simple and natural as possible.'

Mr. Knightley coolly replied, 'My idea of the simple and the natural will be to have the table spread in the dining-room.' Now it was delightful to have Mrs. Elton snubbed, so far as such a thing was possible, and we know besides that Mr. Knightley had other motives; he knew that poor Mr. Woodhouse would be made ill with unhappiness at the idea of a meal out of doors. And yet purely on a matter of principle I cannot get out of my head the unworthy notion that for once Mr. Knightley was wrong and that insufferable Mrs. Elton was right. To be sure she would have spoiled the party wherever it was, as she did at Box Hill, but—well, I am never wholly easy in my mind about it.

Leaving that particular example on one side, it will be generally admitted that the best picnics are out of doors. I have always felt both envy and admiration for the old golfers of St. Andrews, who did not, as men do nowadays, play out their morning round to the home hole and retire for an excellent lunch to the club-house. No, they stopped and had their snack at the hole that is called the ginger-beer hole to this day, and then off again for their second round. That they drank only ginger beer I do not suggest. They would have said, as Dandie Dinmont did of the claret, 'It's ower cauld for my stomach'; but I am sure they enjoyed their lunch with its *al fresco* jolliness and, in theory at least, I should like to emulate them. I still have ecstatic memories from more than forty years ago of a day's golf on a little course at Macamish, on the shores of Lough Swilly. Some sailed across the Lough from Buncrana, others drove innumerable miles from Portsalon: everyone brought his own lunch and we ate it on the edge of a putting green under the lee of a sand-hill in blissful peace and solitude.

Solitude is essential to the full enjoyment of a picnic.

This is a point on which even the most unselfish sometimes belie their beautiful natures. As for those whose
natures are less beautiful, is there any hatred deeper and
more venomous than that which we feel for a rival party
that has had the effrontery to choose the very same place?
It was only lately that I was taken on a picnic to a most
enchanting spot, on the shores of a little lake, secluded,
bowered in woods. And there, on the other side of the
lake to be sure, was another party already encamped.
They were wholly quiet and innocuous, they did us not
the faintest harm: it was their audacity in being there at
all that was so hard to bear. If scowls could have killed
across the water, they would not long have survived, and
doubtless they directed the same malignant glances at us.
I said I was taken on a picnic, and I carefully chose my
words, for a picnic requires considerable energy and
organizing ability, neither of which I possess. That picnic
basket which disgorges an endless wealth of good things
must be a fairy basket. And yet, in point of prosaic fact,
somebody has had to cut the sandwiches and fill the
thermos and pack the bottles of beer and not forget the
opener and do all the other benevolent things which we
are too apt to take for granted. And sometimes the most
dreadful mistakes are innocently made, which threaten
to wreck the picnic.

I have vivid memories of a picnic party up the river at
Cambridge when someone had blundered and made the
tea, in a thermos, with the sugar irrevocably in it. If
there was one thing my father hated more than another
it was sugar in his tea, and, though he was normally
sweet-tempered, this was almost more than he could
endure. I can still hear him protesting in a tone of deep-
est gloom that he did not mind the tea in itself: 'What
I mind is the folly of it.'

The size of a picnic is a matter of individual taste. I cannot wholly agree with the too hospitable Mr. Weston (also in *Emma*) that 'such schemes as these are nothing without numbers'. I am disgracefully inclined to hold that this policy of the more the merrier is a one that can be overdone. Picnics on a large scale can be very good fun, but they demand strong nerves. I remember to have heard that the illustrious family of the Graces used once every summer to have a mighty nutting party, in which the whole clan, and they were essentially clannish, used to sweep across Gloucestershire, forty or fifty strong, sisters, cousins, and aunts, in an irresistible flood. It has, and no doubt it made, a jolly sound. The Doctor himself would have been in his kindest, friendliest and most cheerful mood. And yet my mind misgives me that, at any rate for a stranger, it might have been just a little prostrating.

I confess that there is one great man with whom I should like to go on a great picnic, and that is Dickens. He was filled, I am sure, with the very spirit of picnic. We have only to think of two or three that he describes, that in Mr. Wardle's carriage at the Chatham review, the shooting lunch near Bury when Mr. Pickwick took too much cold punch, and Dora's birthday party. There are no doubt others that I have not thought of, but those three will serve. With what inimitable gusto he would have made the party go! He would have organized every-thing to perfection and made wine cellars in hollow trees. For all I know he would have sung comic songs after lunch. Yes, and made us sing them too. He would have made us do all manner of things that we should have believed ourselves to detest, and for that once we should have loved them. He would have swept us clean off our feet into rapturous enjoyment, and when we woke next day we should have felt that the picnic had been a dream and we had been bewitched.

That picnic being unattainable save in Elysian fields, I cast my unadventurous vote for the small, select and peaceful variety. If I dare to describe briefly two of my own favourites, let not the reader be angry but rather let him translate my words into terms of his own doubtless far superior picnics, and do his private gloating as it were by proxy. My first is an exceedingly select one as it consists, as a rule, only of two roysterers, myself and another, though there has once or twice been a third. It used to take place regularly once and often twice a year and was part of a solemn rite, which I am conscious of having described elsewhere, the drive to Wales. Everything was done according to a strict tradition, and the lunch on Bromyard Common was as unvarying as the 'elevenses'—a glass of beer, and that the 'genuine stunning'—at Broadway. It was not merely on Bromyard Common, which is a large and noble expanse; it was on a particular piece of turf by the side of a particular piece of the road, soon after it passes through a particular piece of woodland; I could find my way blindfold to it at this moment. Sometimes on a fine day we could sit upon the grass; sometimes we must stay in the car. That was the only difference. The sandwiches were always of the same scrumptious quality, and, for no precise reason save that we had done so once, we always washed them down with perry—a drink in my mind solely associated with this festival. Whatever were our other topics of conversation, we tried to recall the name of the inn in Bromyard (yes, now, after an effort, I have remembered it) at which we must take a sharp turn. I am ashamed to think how regularly I expressed the wish to let loose a golfing architect on that gorsy, undulating stretch, clearly designed by Providence for one end. If we concealed any remnants of our meal (though I hope we packed them all up tidily in the car) then I am very sure that it was in the heart of the very same bush. We may never be able to go that journey again, but if ever we do, then, touching wood, I know where we shall lunch. It would be far better to starve than break so sacred a tradition.

My other very particular picnic is of quite recent memory and happened but once; yet it was so enchanting that I cannot for the life of me refrain. This too was within sight of a golf course, not imaginary this time, but a very real one, for it was on the Pebble Ridge at Westward Ho! I suppose it broke one of the regular rules, whether Mrs. Elton's or any one else's, that a picnic should be in the shade, for a blazing sun beat full upon us. Neither did we sit on soft, caressing turf, but on the hard stones of that famous ridge. I remember that on that very day the great J. H. Taylor told us how when he was a boy the ridge had been so tall and steep that it must be scaled on hands and knees. Time has mysteriously mitigated these rigours, for the five of us clambered up comfortably enough, and once we were there the stones made kindly resting places for baskets and glasses and bottles. To find an entirely lonely piece of coast in high midsummer is something to be grateful for, and that was our happy lot. We were as Byron on Sunium's 'marbled steep':

> *Where nothing, save the waves and I,*
> *May hear our mutual murmurs sweep.*

Our own murmurs were louder than those of the waves, which made but the gentlest lapping; yet the air was filled with the great, vague sound of the sea, and such a blue and shining sea. And when we had eaten all the sandwiches we threw stones at some mark on the beach below, in a heaven of laziness and digestion.

It may be that a truly scientific and analytical student would put in different categories picnics which are the sole object of a 'party of pleasure' and those which are, however pleasant, merely incidental to a journey. I have no claims to such depressing epithets, and having let my pen run on at random in the realms of memory, I will draw no such distinctions. Some may be better than others, but all picnics possess an essential beauty and romance, and any true lover, as he falls on his first sandwich, will never fail to say his grace, in Mr. Wardle's words at Chatham, 'Now an't this capital?'

RICHARD CHURCH

Litter Bugs

MANY PEOPLE are uneasy about the latest legislation directed against the activities of the litter bug. Certainly, it is a bad thing to have too many laws, and to introduce any narrowly confined to a specific purpose. There is always the danger of bringing our English Common Law into contempt, and increasing the temptations to evade it. That would be the end of our way of life, for in the long run law can be superseded only by tyranny and bureaucracy.

But surely the uneasiness should be not about the introduction of the law to control untidy people, but about the fact that it has been so badly needed; for it is indeed long overdue. I sometimes think we are the dirtiest people in Europe, especially in public. This is so puzzling because we pride ourselves on our native cleanliness, and it is a common sight to see British tourists abroad fussing over their food, their beds, their seats in public vehicles.

I recall that when investigations were made into the conditions in the catering trade when it was proposed to bring it within the scope of the Trade Board Acts, the disclosures were horrifying. Premises and methods of unmitigated squalor were revealed. Conditions even today are not up to Continental standards. Somehow or other the latest and smartest cafés manage to look grubby after a few months.

Only the other day at three o'clock in the afternoon I

saw a figure emerge with a pail from a side door in one of London's largest and most popular hotels. She was extremely dirty—clothes, hands, face and legs. She emptied her pail of slops along the gutter, wiped the back of her hand across her nose, shook the bucket in the air, and leisurely returned to earth, while the swill trickled along the gutter beneath the parked cars.

But our lack of kitchen cleanliness is a matter that could be discussed indefinitely. I still prefer to eat in France or Tuscany. Meanwhile, our national oddity in other forms of so-called cleanliness has increased to such proportions that legislation has had to be made to bring it under control.

Will the new law work? Or is the couldn't-care-less attitude so deeply ingrained that nothing will change our national habits? Visitors from abroad, who during the past four or five centuries have recorded their impressions of our way of life, have always remarked upon our unaccountable habits in public, just as they have noted what they call 'the insolence' of our domestic servants, and our general laziness and tolerance of slackness. So present-day conditions are nothing new.

With the rapid increase in population, the easy way of conducting ourselves in public tends to create chaos. One pair of lovers strolling through a pretty woodland scene only enhances the prospect. Even if the young man throws down an empty cigarette carton behind a bush, the beauty of the scene is but little impoverished. But if five hundred couples pass through that wood, and dispose casually of their packagings, what is the result?

The answer, of course, is taken for granted by many people. But the trouble is, that there are other folk who have something lacking in their make-up. They would not even be conscious of a problem here. What do we call them? Are they Philistines, barbarians? But they might well be decent, honest, well-meaning persons, who would be shocked if we attacked them, enraged by the filth they are leaving behind. Is it merely a matter of aesthetics? Just as some people are tone-deaf and cannot distinguish a Beethoven symphony from *Rule Britannia*, so these people seem to be unconscious of creating a nuisance when they throw an ice-cream carton on the turf in a beauty-spot, or chuck a broken bedstead into the village pond. Perhaps these despoilers of the street and the countryside are like people in the advertisements for breath purifiers, blandly indifferent to the caption that 'your best friends will not tell you'.

We must tell these litter bugs. We have got to try to bring home to them the heinousness of their habits. That is what the new law intends. But will it succeed?

I am not hopeful. The most difficult job in the world is to awaken those minds to certain facts or ideas outside the range of their consciousness. Take the children, for instance. All children are untidy, and even personally dirty. They have to be made to wash themselves, and taught to be methodical about the house.

The responsibility lies with their parents, especially their mothers. It is no easy task for the women of this country, because the tradition of home discipline has been influenced by the laxity of American homes. Mothers should take it for granted that their children must learn to be habitually tidy in the small things of life; cleaning up after their games, rounding off every job. It helps to shape the fabric of their minds and characters. The fight against the litter bug should begin in the nursery and the kitchen; a difficult task but a valuable part of social education.

The task becomes still more difficult when it attacks

E

the conduct of children out of doors. I live in a country hamlet near a boarding school which is conducted excellently. But every day some of the boys come up to the village store and buy sweets, ices, fruit pies and other things packed in cartons, silver paper, Cellophane. I watch, and watch in agony, a couple or more of them strolling back, consuming their tuck. I know that as they pass the triangle of well-groomed lawn where the two lanes meet outside my house, one of them, in the course of conversation over the all-important things of boyhood, will drop that carton or wrapper on my lawn without even looking round, or being conscious of what he is doing.

Am I justified in longing to rush out, turn that boy up, and give him a vigorous touch of the bastinado on the soles of his indifferent feet? He is most probably a decent youngster, working hard at school, intent on his future career and all the rest of the social virtues. But he is a litter bug.

What about the adults? What are we to do about them? Oh the irony of it! I have known dustmen come to collect the domestic waste, and in the process to throw down near the house an empty matchbox or cigarette package. There it lies, in the centre of the road between the hedgerows, overhung by honeysuckle or wild roses, an eyesore to every civilized passer-by. But how many *are* civilized in this respect?

It is most depressing to realize that vast numbers of our British community do not care a damn, are not even aware of the incongruity and filthiness of this indiscriminate chucking away of what they do not want. Perfectly respectable people do it. That is the trouble. How can we wake them up to their crime? It defames the beauty of our land, disturbs the equanimity of the rest of the community, and in the end costs an enormous amount of money. Is it generally known that the London County Council spend £12,000 a year on collecting litter from the royal parks alone?

Is it due to a lack of the spirit of reverence? Is it the reverse side of the medal of democratic independence, a kind of derisive gesture against all authority? Sometimes I am inclined to be so pessimistic that I believe in positive evil, a power that makes certain people eager to destroy beauty when confronted by it. Grandeur, nobility, immaculateness, these are qualities that wake the Caliban in some folk. Even sanctity is not secure against their depradations. They will drop their sordid litter under the dome of St. Paul's Cathedral, or in front of the altar in an ancient village church.

I noticed only a few weeks ago that on the fine floor of the new Planetarium in London (a most beautiful functional interior, the very temple of pure mathematics) there were cartons and scraps of toffee paper, matches and other debris. Yet the audience in this place must at least have come with the glimmerings of controlled and enlightened intelligence!

In my despair, I have sometimes longed for power to seize such litter bugs on the spot, and to have them branded on the cheek, or at least on their garments, with a blazoning of 'L'. Would that put them to shame, as passers-by looked the other way after seeing this infamous initial? Would they at last wake up to the fact that they are malefactors, destroyers of the country to which they imagine themselves to be so loyal?

Such drastic methods are not to be adopted, but substantial fines, and possible imprisonment for wilful and incessant offenders, are now within the power of the magistrates. In many countries, policemen are able to fine on the spot. We do not want this dangerous precedent for further imposition on the freedom of the citizen. Nor do we want to add unduly to the penal code. Prevention rather than punishment is the ideal to strive after. How is that possible but by education, and a permanent form of education that goes down into the depths of the mind, so that taste for aesthetic rightness is created?

But there will always remain the human being whose aesthetic sense remains as limited as that shown by the ape or the young child. He (and she) has to be controlled. Let us hope that the new law may be a useful instrument to that end.

HUNTER DAVIES

The Newsvendor

THE NEWSVENDOR'S stall was outside a tube station in a
busy part of London, not far from the City. But for most
of the afternoon he had been just standing around doing
nothing. Now the steady trickle of office workers, which
had begun around four, started to turn into a torrent.
For the next one and a half hours he worked like a
demon. During this time, he sold almost 5,000 copies of
the *Evening Standard* and the *Evening News*, roughly
one every second.

As usual, he and his cousin (his regular assistant) had
been joined for the evening rush by his wife and a boy.
The boy fed the other three with papers.

There was no time for back chat or conversation. In
one action, the three of them grabbed money and shoved
out papers. Customers who were slow or hesitant missed
their turn and were ignored, other customers being served
over and around them. When eventually they got their
money ready and decided what they wanted, they were
served quickly and icily.

'You're ready, are you then, madam?' said the Newsvendor, to a woman who had been fumbling for some
time with a purseful of change. 'I thought at least you
was going to make a takeover bid.'

At six-thirty, with the worst over, the Newsvendor at
last spared a breath for sarcasm.

He was a neat, clean, casually dressed man, of about
forty. He had a rather serious, humourless face. He

53

didn't speak much to the customers or his helpers, but when he did, he spoke slowly and quietly, as if to himself.

The Newsvendor's line was efficiency, not repartee. The office workers, rushing in a lemming-like frenzy from his stall to their tubes, appreciated his speed.

It had been a good day. There had been a big air crash overnight which had sold many extra morning papers. Lunch-time had been warm and sunny. Many people had therefore been walking around, buying magazines to read outside with their sandwiches.

Now it was cold and there was a slight drizzle. People preferred the tube to the bus, so his custom rose. They wanted an evening paper for a cheerless journey ahead and a depressing evening indoors.

The Newsvendor started to collect the money together. He tied it in blue Bank bags, carefully counting and re-checking. Then he and his wife left the stall. It was the assistant's turn to look after it till eight o'clock, when it would be packed away for the night.

His large white Jaguar was parked nearby. It was in the private car park of a large Government building. He'd parked it there for six months, pretending to be part of a central heating firm working in the building. They would get wise to him soon and he'd have to look for parking meters again, which was ridiculous. The prices were extortionate.

A couple of junior clerks, regular customers who'd bought papers from him that evening, happened to see him getting into his big car.

'Must be a lot of money in papers, eh?' one of them shouted.

He just smiled coldly in reply, and got into the car, placing the bags of money on the floor.

He had just under £70 in assorted notes and change.

His day's takings. It was slightly above average. Usually it was around £50. On a really good day, it could be as high as £100.

He thought about the two clerks on the way home. Like the majority of his customers, despite their white shirts and dark suits, they probably made in a week as much as he could make in a good day.

He got home to his house in South London. It was a semi-detached, post-war house, furnished expensively in modern furniture, but not flashily. The only sign in his living-room of more than usual affluence was a large, well-stocked, gaily decorated, illuminated bar. It dominated one corner. Spanish bull-fighting posters covered the wall behind it.

He stood behind the bar after his supper, slowly drinking beer, while his wife and his only child, a boy of twenty-one, watched TV.

'My stall has been in my family for eighty-five years,' he said quietly and flatly. 'Passed on from father to son. Most street stalls are like that. I'm very proud of it. I want it to go on. Some of my customers remember my grandmother. That means something.

'I first went down there and started helping when I was ten. They still talk in the family about how it happened. I was the eldest and had the cheek to complain that we never got no Sunday breakfast. This was because on Saturday nights they'd be out boozing all night and sleep all Sunday morning. We don't do no Sunday papers. My Dad said that if I started work every morning at six, *I'd* want to sleep in on my day off. So I said OK. Let me start work as well at six, then I'd see, wouldn't I.

'So from the age of ten I started working on the stall. Every morning from six till eight.

'We used to have lots of deliveries to hotels in those

days. I'd do this till eight then have breakfast in a taxi cab shelter. After school, I'd go back to the stall again and work till seven in the evening.

'I enjoyed it. It was more like a market in them days. There were all sorts of other street stalls as well. Flower sellers, barrow boys, matchbox men. All the lot.

'I was quite good at school. I liked it. At school, I was like a millionaire. I got five bob a week pocket money, that was for working on the stall really. Some married men weren't making that money. I remember carrying one boy to school on my back because he had no shoes.

'I left school at thirteen. It was really because the war broke out. All the schools had closed and there was none to go to. Otherwise I might have stayed at school longer.

'I went straight to the stall and worked there full time for two years.

'Then one day I was delivering to this hotel when I got talking to a ship's steward who was staying there. He said he was going back to Bristol that evening. Why didn't I come with him?

'So I went back to the stall and left a message for my Mum that I wouldn't be coming back, I'd gone to sea. That was how I joined the Merchant Navy. I was fifteen and a half.

'My first trip was to New York. It lasted six weeks. I wrote home to my Mum, but in them days they used to take foreign stamps off before they were delivered so no one knew where you were. When I did come back, no one ever believed I'd been to New York.

'I loved the Merchant Navy. As a kid I'd always been potty about ships. When other kids were collecting train numbers, I used to sit at the Thames collecting tug boat numbers. I had a mania for it, you could say. I went on the *Discovery* so many times it was ridiculous. I knew it backwards.

'On September 3, 1943, the boat I was on got sunk. It was a hospital ship coming from Palermo. I got picked up OK.

'I came out in 1947, when I was twenty-one. I didn't really want to. I did it for the family and the stall.

'During the war, my mother looked after it. My father had died and, being the eldest, I'd inherited the stall. My mother had been looking after it till I came of age.

'In 1947, newspapers were going to come off the ration at last, so that would mean a lot more work for her. So I felt I had to come back to take over the stall.

'There was lots of queues with the rationing, sometimes 100 yards long and three deep. But no money. I was making more in the Merchant Navy. But once rationing came off, there was a lot more money to be made.

'Until the last two years, I've worked every week-day from six in the morning till seven at night. Now three mornings a week, Mondays, Tuesdays and Wednesdays, I start late, at nine. It mucks up your social life if you have to start at six every morning.

'We pack up at ten on Saturdays. There's nobody around. All the offices in the City and West End are on a five-day week these days.

'I designed the stall myself, the shade as well. I got fed up buying stuff from people who never worked a stall.

'We leave it on the pavement at night. The Council could be naughty and stop me if they wanted, but it would be such a bother putting it anywhere else. I leave all the magazines inside. They haven't been nicked yet.

Once or twice been broken into, just by kids playing around.

'I get fifty quire of morning papers. There's twenty-six in a quire, so that's 1,300. Mostly *Express* and *Mirrors*, then *Telegraphs*, *Financial Times*, *Mail* and *Sun*. I get about 160 quire of Evenings.

'It's usually about the same number. Wyman's, my agents, box them out if something good's happened—if President Kennedy was assassinated they'd automatically send me more copies without me asking.

'The first thing I do of a morning is arrange the stall. I'm very particular about this. I won't sell nothing till everything's all arranged. I just tell people to go away. Come back in half an hour when I'm ready, then I'll sell you something. They're usually very good, even say they were sorry for bothering me earlier.

'I also check all the quires first thing. You'd be amazed how many papers get knocked off, just odd ones here and there. They make a lot of money these drivers and boys and inside men, but they're the biggest lot of rogues ever. It's one of my biggest worries that, checking the quires.

'Then I get my orders ready. I don't do so much these days, just a few big offices and hotels. I gave a lot up, not worth the trouble. I used to do some barristers. Trail up five flights of steps. Lovely people. But they never paid their bills. Had to wait months and months. So I packed it in.

'My best order is for a press cutting agency. This Yank just come up to me one day and said could I send him one copy of every paper. I took them, and he said, I thought I said one of each? Turned out he meant one of each edition!

'I had to chase them all up. I didn't know there were

so many. There's thirteen editions each morning of the *Daily Express* for a start. The most is the *News of the World*—nineteen editions. All my life in papers, I never knew about these editions.

'When I've made the orders up, I take fifteen minutes off about seven-fifteen to deliver them. I just wait till somebody I know goes by or get one of the station staff to keep an eye on the stall.

'Then the morning rush starts from about eight, and goes on till ten. I take £10 in just those two hours.

'Those two hours are hectic. There's a paper shop, not twenty yards away inside the tube station. We don't just do better than them. We pulverize them.

'Most shops say the street sellers take their trade away, but I like to think it's the other way round. In my father's day, the steam trains used to use the station and the whole place was different and there was no shop there. So we were here first. They've taken our trade.

'At nine o'clock, if it's me on early, my cousin comes on. We start checking over the morning papers and money as soon as we can, before the first editions of the evenings start. I like to keep them separate. You can keep an eye on mistakes and thieving better.

'At ten o'clock, I take the overnight money and the morning money to the bank, in loose change. You don't get so much coppers today. There'd be £18-£20 of coppers in the old days. Now it's only £6 or £7. Everybody wants coppers. The bank manager's waiting for us to bring them. It's all these funny prices—teas fivepence and rolls sevenpence round our area. They always need coppers.

'You can get a rash from coppers if you're not careful, so I always keep very clean. I've seen one bloke who'd been rubbing his face with his hands, come out something horrible. So I've taught myself never to touch my face when I'm working.

'The evenings come in just after nine-thirty. I don't sell many first editions now. The betting shops have them up on the walls for free.

'Things are pretty slow up to twelve o'clock, then it works up a bit, especially if it's fine. If it's bad, they all stay in their offices and it's just me and the pigeons outside.

'Things are slow again from two to three-thirty, then at four you get the first home people. Then of course from five to six-thirty, it's very fast and we work like bloody lunatics.

'I start counting up the money at six-thirty. I've never known it right all my life. Fact, I've never known it in our favour. But unless it's not more than ten bob out, we don't worry. If it's over that, we have a court enquiry and decide who's nicking papers.

'All stalls are different, with different busy times and things. I can only talk for me. I'm probably pretty average for a tube stall in what we sell. Nothing like the best—nothing like Regent Street or Piccadilly.

'The two mad rushes make up for the slow times. So speed is essential. Other stalls have more time to be sociable. I'm not interested in their health or saying hello, just in getting the money out of their hands. Slow, dithery women drive me mad, holding everything up. You get in rhythm of selling and you don't want anything to stop it.

'You try to hurry people into decision. Embarrass them by calling out, Can I help you Sir? You mustn't let them read the papers.

'You've got to watch them with *Playboy*. They try to look at it on the stall without paying. It costs 8s. 6d. I can't sell it if it's dirty. People are entitled to a clean one. They're just trying to have a free look at the nudes, so you do a double somersault to stop them. You say, what do you think this is, a bleeding library?

'I know most of my customers, at least ninety per cent of them. Once they come to you, they tend to stick. Even the dirtiest, scruffiest seller has his fans.

'I can tell the time of day by the customers. The char-ladies are first at six, all swearing like troopers. I've known a lot of them since I was a boy.

'Then the post office workers start coming, then the first of the office staff. The barristers don't come till nine-thirty.

'I don't care much for the postmen as customers. They're all on different shifts and some start before I'm here. No. I wouldn't call them an asset.

'My best customers are girls. Nearly every one of them spends about six or seven shillings a week each, mainly on women's magazines. They're the ones I really try to keep happy. I talk to them if I can. Try to find out their Christian names.

'The girls are much better than the men. The men have got commitments and can't afford much. Any money the girls have is just pocket money. It doesn't matter to them. If a man spends 1s. 6d. on a magazine, he thinks he's keeping you.

'You get a lot of rude people, just throw the money at you as if you had a disease and they didn't want to get near. Others don't know what they want and poke around till you could strangle them. Then there's always some who want the paper at the bottom of the pile because he thinks you're hiding all the late ones.

'The people I hate most of all are the Welsh. It's their meanness I don't like. They're all double eyed. Everything about them is rotten. They just want to talk about 1926 all the time. I know you could introduce me to some and I'd have to say they were quite nice people, but I've found on the whole I don't like Welsh people. I suppose you could call it my peculiarity.

'I've seen punch-ups and lovers quarrelling. A woman jumped into the Thames while her lover and her husband were fighting each other. Excuse me, I said to the husband, but your wife has just jumped into the Thames. He just stood there and the lover dived in.

'I've seen a bloke of six foot six stand in tears in front of me, with his hands all swollen up. He'd just half killed someone who's gone off with his wife.

'You can see the expression on lovers' faces. You can tell when the girl is going to cry.

'But the atmosphere isn't the same, now the barrow boys have gone. We had some marvellous times with them. The hot chestnut seller was always having everybody on. It was laughter all day long. It really was. Time does hang now.

'I dislike the long hours, and I've now got a bit scared of a cold winter. It never used to worry me, till that cold winter three years ago.

'The office clerks tend to look down upon you, as if they were better than you. The barristers are OK. They're toffs.

'My biggest worry is what I said, watching the quires. You have to watch the reps and boys like bloody hawks. You'd never think it to talk to them, they're all smart dressers, butter wouldn't melt in their mouths. But they've all got some fiddle. When you accuse them, they always have the same answer. We never took them—it must be the machine's fault.

'What sells papers is bad news. Nobody's interested in

good news. Sport stories don't sell much extra papers, or politics. Bad news and scandal. That's what you want.

'I remember the Duke of Windsor's abdication. It was like a madhouse on our stall. I was just a boy helping my Dad. He got pinned up against the wall by the crowds. He just stood there screaming at me for more papers.

'The *Flying Enterprise*, that was very good indeed. Surprising, really. It was a running story, sold papers all during the day, everybody wanted to know what was happening.

'Kennedy of course was good. And the Profumo affair. That was the best scandal I can remember.

'Churchill's death wasn't as good as it could have been, what with him hanging on so long and being so old. Now, if it had been all sudden, that would have been a newsvendor's dream. But we did well with his funeral.

'Bill posters don't sell papers, at least I don't think so. Some do.

'You get five bob for every poster you have up, but I don't think it's worth it. A bit of wind, and you're picking them up and down out the gutter all day. The minute you get fed up, the rep comes along and says I'm not paying you five bob a week for nothing, get that board up.

'Mind you, you can make a lot of money from them. I know one stall where he has forty posters—that's £10 a week for a start. You can't see his stall for them.

'I've only had one hard time on the stall, that was during the newspaper strike. I must have been looking pretty miserable 'cos one customer said if I came with him, he'd put in a good word for me and I could work with him. He was a lift operator. He said I'd get £11 a week if I was lucky. Thank God things have never got that bad.

'About three years ago I began to get really ambitious and I decided to buy another stall. I thought it would be a good investment, for my son as much as for me.

'I made a lot of money from it and bought a bungalow in Essex.

'I decided on Essex because if I bought another house in London the income tax people might wonder where I was getting all the money from. I don't pay income tax, you see. I thought, moving out of London they wouldn't find out.

'I only officially put down £75 deposit on the house, but the income tax were still on to me. Wanted to know if I wasn't earning enough to pay tax, how could I afford £75. Which is pretty stupid. Anybody can lay their hands on £75 these days.

'But it just shows you. Most street boys are like me, careful and suspicious. Well you have to be, because you should never underestimate anybody. While I'm scheming against them, I always think they'll be scheming against me.

'I don't have an accountant. I know all the tricks myself. I've had a lifetime on the streets, haven't I?

'But my wife fell ill and it was awkward for us travelling all that way in every day, though we loved the country. So we came back into London. We made £1,000 selling the Essex house. This one cost us £5,000. It's now worth £8,500, going by what others have gone for.

'With my wife not being able to help as much, I decided to sell the other stall. Staff was difficult to get as well. You make a lot of money on the stalls, but it's long hours and people don't like that.

'I suppose I make a clear profit of £50 a week. That's what I get myself. I pay all the bills personally, and give my wife £16 a week for the housekeeping. That really includes £4 a week which she gets for working on the stall. It's supposed to be for her own things, like getting her hair done.

'We don't like a lot of show. We just have the sort of comforts most people have these days, fridges, central heating, a bar, that sort of thing.

'We're like most street boys. Money doesn't matter all that much. Easy come and easy go. We worry about tomorrow when tomorrow comes.

'The most important thing in my life is my home—my wife and my son. If they're happy, I'm happy.

'I never used to go out drinking till recently. Always been a home loving boy. But as my son has been getting older, he goes out with his own friends. We used to have some good times together. I bought him a Go-Kart. I've now bought him his own car, a new Ford, so it's easy for him to go out on his own.

'So now my wife and I go out drinking together. Not to pubs. We go to clubs. Not working men's clubs. Social clubs, nice ones. We go three or four times a week. On a Saturday night, oh, I don't know, we might spend £10. Depends on the mood we're in.

'But we don't live expensively. We've always got fun out of easy things.

'We always go abroad touring for our holidays, in the car. We're off to Italy this year for three weeks. It's the tenth year we've been there.

'I'm a bit funny about the car. I never clean it myself. I don't like to, so I pay to get it done. But I clean inside the car. You should see the engine. It's lovely and clean.

'I don't have much extravagances. I just have about

F

ten suits, oh, and two more in the tailor's. Not very expensive, about £30 each.

'When we're on our holidays, we don't go in bed and breakfast or guest houses, but in good hotels. Two star hotels, not three, because that might be a bit out of our depth.

'So really, with all these worries, I've made my son have two strings to his bow. He's next in line for my business and I want him to take it over, but I think he should be able to do something else as well, just in case.

'So I told him he should learn a trade before coming into the business. I let him choose. One day he said he'd like to be a bricklayer, so I got him started.

'There's all this talk about boys not wanting to take a trade these days, but the trouble I had getting him in. Eventually, I pulled a few strings and gave a few quid out here and there, and I got him apprenticed. It's ridiculous. The youth of England want to have a trade, but they can't get in.

'He's doing very well. He's now studying for his Higher National. He can come into the business when he's finished, if he wants to.

'I suppose, myself, I'll keep on as long as I can. We often think, the wife and me, it would be nice to buy a country pub. But that's just one of our harebrain schemes.

'It would be some sort of security, preparing ourselves for the future in case anything happened to the stall. But I like the stall, and I like working in the open air. And I'm awfully proud of my stall, eighty-five years from father to son, it's a long time.

'I'll probably work on the stall till I drop. You have to in this game. There's no pension or sick pay. If you're sick, you have to pay somebody to look after the stall. So you're never sick.

'I'm against the National Health Scheme. I hate it. And all that Insurance for the self-employed. You have to pay too much.

'I've never missed a day since the war. When I've a cold or 'flu, I still go to work. The longest I've been off was half a day, when I had a slipped disc. I did it lifting my car. I went round these osteopaths till I got one to click it into place, and I went back to work.

'The Welfare State is all wrong. We have to look after ourselves, why shouldn't others? People with no initiative get led around like little boys. They should get no help at all.

'The whole scheme of wages is all wrong. The lazy people should get paid nothing. The brainy and the initiative should get it all.

'There are a few exceptions. I agree nurses are worth more than £10 a week, or whatever they get. They should get £50, anything in fact, there's no limit to what nurses deserve. But you couldn't do it. If you made it £50 a week, it wouldn't just be the dedicated women who wanted to be nurses. You'd get little flopsies just doing it for the money. So that wouldn't work, would it?

'I think in most cases it is laziness why people don't work hard enough. Look at roadsweepers; people think it's because they're really a bit slow and stupid. They're not. They're crafty, the way babies are crafty. I have to give the roadsweeper two bob before he sweeps under my stall.

'I think the postmen who work on the counters in post offices shouldn't get tuppence a week. Every time I go in I have to wait twenty minutes. What would happen if my customers had to wait twenty minutes?

'They should be on a commission, then the lazy ones wouldn't get anything. So should bus crews, the driver and the conductor working together. They would be paid according to how many fares they took. Wouldn't it be nice to run for a bus and know they'd wait for you?

'It works with asphalters, why not other people? They get paid for how much they lay. Look how hard they work.

'No, the system's all wrong. People should only get paid what they're worth.

'I don't believe in income tax. No one likes paying it, ninety-nine out of 100 try to evade it, claiming anything they can think of. Why should I pay any? I can look after myself, let the others look after themselves. I'd be paying half what I earned if I wasn't careful. I like to make money. I want to get hold of as much of it as possible.

'I'm against children's allowances. People should stand on their own two feet. If they can't support children, they shouldn't have them. Now old age pensioners, they should definitely have more money.

'M.P.s they're not worth tuppence. I've met them and I wonder how they get their jobs.

'I don't think teachers and doctors are all that important, not like nurses. Some are bad, some are good.

'People have lost the will to work because of this Welfare State. You take something back to a shop because it's bad and do they apologize and try to help? Do they, huh. They just laugh and say, so what.

'There's a big post office building near my stall, with about 5,000 people. Every minute of the day the canteen is absolutely packed and so is the roof. Who's doing all the work?

'Maybe I'm just jealous. I have to work hard for my money, using my own initiative and ability.

'I'm a 100 per cent Conservative. A True Blue Tory.

I'm not ashamed about that. I'll tell anybody. I'm awfully proud of it.

'To me, the country is like a big shop. So, it should be businessmen that's running it. Labour are no good. They're all loud mouthed Trade Unionists.

'O.K. so I've just got a 2½d. stall. But, say I branched out, got more stalls and employed twelve people, worked bloody hard. One day they'd form a union and tell *me* how to run it.

'You've no legal right to your pitch, but they can change hands for a lot of money. The other stall I used to have, I sold it for £850. I've just heard of one outside Victoria that went for £5,000. I was just told, I don't know. But I can believe it. There's a lot of money there, probably worth every penny of it.

'But everybody with a stall at a station is worried. I knew one bloke at Kings Cross. They changed the front overnight and his stall was gone.

'I don't believe in the Church, though I suppose I'm Church of England. It's O.K. for weddings, christenings and funerals.

'Now, the Catholics, I think that's a most wonderful religion. It's sincere. That's what it is. I've often thought of being a convert, but my wife's against it.

'Most religious bodies come round to see us on the stall at some time. I suppose they think we need it, all starving with our feet out of our boots.

'The Catholics are the only ones I can talk to. The others just talk stoopid. That's all I can describe it. Stoopid. Their conversation doesn't make sense. The Catholics are different. I can understand them. They go drinking with you. Without being, I don't know, funny.

'The Church of England just has a different attitude.

Their clergymen are very uninteresting. The life has
gone out of them. They're not there.

'I consider my job worthwhile. If my newspaper is late
coming through my letter box at home in the morning,
I walk up and down looking for it and get annoyed.
When I'm late with my orders, people say to me, how
dare you be late. People *want* their papers, you see. So
it must be worthwhile. I like to think I am important.

'Not that I've any interest in newspapers, personally.
I never read them. I often say to my wife, I don't know
why people buy the bloody papers, there's nothing in
them.'

SIR HAROLD NICOLSON

The Future of the Public Schools

I HAVE been reading a pamphlet by Mr. J. H. Simpson, Principal of the College of St. Mark and St. John, which throws an interesting sidelight upon the problem of our Public Schools. Mr. Simpson was for twelve years headmaster of a small boarding-school, in which the majority of pupils came from working-class, or lower middle-class, homes. He is thus one of the few men who have had direct and prolonged experience of the effect of the boarding-school system upon the working-class boy. His views, for this reason, merit every attention. His argument is based upon the assumption that, whereas a few Public Schools may be able for some years to survive the New Economic Order, most of them will be unable to maintain themselves without financial assistance from the State. He asks whether such assistance would be justified, or in other words whether the taxpayer would obtain a really useful return for his money. He therefore addresses himself to the problem of whether the virtues and advantages taught or provided by our Public Schools could, by some readjustment of our educational machinery, be rendered available to children in the lower income groups. This leads him to an examination of these advantages and to the consideration whether in fact they could be transferred or transmitted to the boys and girls of the elementary day school.

Mr. Simpson asserts that there are seven main virtues

or advantages which are generally associated with the
Public School system. The man who has had the privilege
of a Public School education is generally free from feelings of social inferiority, is more confident and assured in
his dealings with his fellow-men, and is 'less prone to
certain mean habits of thought and action which come
from an attitude towards life which is primarily defen-
sive'. Enjoying as he does the advantages of a compara-
tively cultured home, he becomes more adept in the art
of living. In the course of his training he acquires a sense
of responsibility towards those who are less fortunately
situated than himself. The Public School boy, moreover,
inherits a long religious tradition, acquires pride in his
own school, and learns to act loyally towards his masters
and school-fellows. And, finally, the fact that at a tender
age he is removed from home influence and urban surroundings has a marked, and upon the whole a beneficial,
influence upon his health and character. How many of
these seven advantages, asks Mr. Simpson, are transferable and how many are exclusive? He contends that the
first three (namely, social self-confidence, a cultural home
and responsibility towards the less fortunate) are not
transferable, since they depend not upon any educational
machinery, but upon the present condition of society.
According as income-levels become more uniform these
class distinctions will tend to diminish, and the sense of
responsibility will merge, as it has merged in the United
States, into a diffused social conscience. The next three
advantages (religious tradition, pride and loyalty) will,
without State intervention, be acquired by secondary day
schools once they are able to settle denominational problems and to acquire greater prestige and self-reliance.
Thus of the seven virtues or advantages provided by the
Public School system, three are not transferable and three

are not exclusive. It is in his opinion imprudent to spend large sums of public money upon something which you will never get or upon something which you will acquire in any case. Mr. Simpson concludes, therefore, that 'it is not in the national interest that money should be spent by the State with the direct object of preserving the Public Schools'.

Mr. Simpson's argument is not, however, wholly negative. He is left with his seventh virtue, namely, the advantage derived from the boarding system in itself. He has little doubt that it is of value to a boy (and presumably to a girl also) to be away from home for certain periods before the age of eighteen. He agrees that the rural surroundings, the amenities and the beauty of many of our Public Schools do confer a distinct physical and mental benefit upon those who are privileged to enjoy them. He would like to see those benefits extended to the children of poor parents, although he feels that the four years at present devoted to Public School education are too protracted, and that a year, or even six months, should suffice to meet all requirements. His proposal is therefore that those of the Public Schools which are unable to maintain themselves without State assistance should be turned into 'reception schools' or 'short-period boarding-schools' to which day-school children could be transferred for a certain period of their course. Subject to this exception he would let the Public Schools sink or swim without assistance from the State.

Mr. Simpson's pamphlet is impressive, since it deals objectively and from an unusual angle with a problem which is often blurred either by prejudice or by sentiment. There are those who detest the Public School system because it is to their minds the symbol, and perhaps even the cause, of class distinctions. There are those

whose attitude towards the problem is coloured by sentimental affections and who are unable to approach it with
reason or with calm. If it be wholly true that the Public
School system is the expression of a conscious educational
theory, then it is probable that before the century closes
the whole system will have become an anachronism. As
such, it could scarcely be preserved by subsidies from the
Exchequer. But is this assumption wholly true? It may
well have been a misfortune that the different levels of
our educational system should have tended to coincide
with the different levels of income, rank or status. But
it would be incorrect to assume that our Public Schools
mean nothing more than reserved enclosures in which
the children of the rich are given a luxury education. The
resentment which this assumption has created tempts
people to ignore, or to minimize, the educational value
which the system possesses. In fact, the Seven Virtues
which Mr. Simpson defines, and then eliminates, do not
by any means comprise the total range of advantage
offered by a Public School. There are other valuable
virtues which are taught or absorbed to an extent not
found in any other country or under any other system.
There is the virtue of humility, which is the foundation
of any proper exercise of power; there is tolerance, which
is the companion of reason; under the Public School
system boys learn to differentiate between conceit and
pride, between authority and arrogance, between obedi-
ence and subservience. The very harshness of the system
fortifies character more often than it warps it; and if the
purpose of education be to adjust the individual to the
group, then the processes of adjustment practised at a
Public School are certainly more effective than any which
I have observed abroad. I doubt whether these advantages
are provided to the same extent by any day-school.

I am reminded of a phrase which occurs in Mr. J. F. Roxburgh's little book, *Eleutheros*, 'If,' he wrote in 1930, 'the best of the English Public Schools . . . can select and secure the very best young Englishmen of each generation, this country will begin to build up a new aristocracy of character and capacity such as the world has not hitherto seen.' So far from abolishing the Public Schools or allowing them to perish from inanition, Mr. Roxburgh would open their doors to the best boys from the elementary day-schools. Mr. Simpson would not agree with this suggestion, since he is opposed to the theory that the Public Schools should allot free or special places to boys from elementary day-schools. He points out that this method would mean that the ablest working-class boys were segregated from their fellows at the age of twelve; that the secondary day-schools would thereby be deprived of their most promising material and relegated 'to a recognized second-best'; and that it is doubtful whether the boys thus transplanted would in fact achieve either happiness or self-confidence. I am impressed by this argument, since Mr. Simpson has very special experience of the problem he is discussing. But I hope none the less that when Mr. Butler[1] comes to frame the great Education Act of 1943 he will devise some means by which our Public Schools shall cease to be purely private.

[1] Mr. R. A. Butler, then Minister of Education; later Lord Butler, Master of Trinity College, Cambridge.

A. P. HERBERT

Members' Pay

REGINA *v*. WILPOT, M.P.

(*Before the Lord Chief Justice and the Judges of the High Court sitting* in banc.)

THE LORD CHIEF JUSTICE today gave judgment in this important case concerning the recent increase in the remuneration of Members of Parliament. He said:

This is in the nature of a test case which the Court has considered at the request of the Speaker of the House of Commons. The defendant, Mr. Henry Wilpot, was elected to the House of Commons by the delighted citizens of Burbleton (West) in 1952. At that time the annual sum received by Members of Parliament—I use that cautious expression for reasons which will appear later—was £1,000 a year. In the present year there have been two or three debates concerning the inadequacy of this sum and the propriety of an increase. It was touching, one witness told the Court, to see what brotherly love and forbearance was shown in these discussions by Members of all parties, who in other subjects are accustomed to address each other as if they were snakes or tigers. It was in the end resolved by a large majority that an increase to £1,500 per annum was desirable and fitting. This decision was accepted and executed by Her Majesty's Government and is now in force. It was proved before us that the defendant has received, and accepted, the first instalment of what the common people would call his 'rise'.

With the ethics of these affairs this Court has nothing to do. Indeed, it would ill become Her Majesty's Judges, who have recently received a belated improvement in their own position, to criticize the Members of Parliament, who also find themselves hardly pressed by the heavy expenditure of the State and the cruel taxes for which they are responsible. Our task is only to interpret the law.

Now, in 1707, in the reign of Queen Anne, was passed the Succession to the Crown Act. Section 25 provides that if any Member of Parliament

> shall accept of any office of profit from the Crown, during such time as he shall continue a member, his election shall be and is hereby declared to be void and a new writ shall issue for a new election, as if such person so accepting, was naturally dead; provided nevertheless that such person shall be capable of being again elected.

The purpose of this arrangement, I think is clear. For one thing, there may be some suspicion of nepotism or corruption, some question of unfitness in the appointment, which the sovereign people at a popular election may examine and condemn. For another—and this perhaps is more important—there has been a drastic change in the relations between the Member and his constituents. They chose a man who could serve them faithfully—and in those days serve for nothing—who would devote to their interests all his time and talents. Now, they find, he has sold his talents, and much of his time, to the Ministers. For all his fine professions at the election, the hope of profit, the greed for power, was hidden in his heart. He may, for all they know, have sacrificed his principles to secure his post. He may have put it out of his power to pursue with vigour the policies, the promises, for which they gave him their votes. Accordingly, they are given this opportunity to call him to account, to elect him again, if they are satisfied, and reject him if they are not.

In this case it is argued that these wholesome precautions ought to apply, and legally do apply, to Mr. Wilpot. Again, there has been a drastic change in his relations with the people of Burbleton (West). They elected one man, and now they have another. Any ordinary man whose annual remuneration is suddenly advanced by a half—and there are not many—at once moves into another world. The defendant, in the box, admitted that at the election he said nothing about the inadequacy of the Parliamentary 'pay', nothing of any intention to press for an increase. On the contrary, according to the evidence, he asked with passionate eagerness to be sent to Parliament, though well aware of the terms and conditions of that employment. He also promised in many ways to secure an improvement in the lot of the poor: but these undertakings, through no fault of his own, perhaps, have not all been fulfilled. Further, the electors are now entitled to suspect that the man they chose for selfless service and philanthropic purpose had all the time in his heart the desire for profit and the intention to pursue it. In these circumstances it is not at all surprising if the electors wish him to vacate his seat and offer himself for election again. The question is, is that the law?

The Attorney-General, who appeared for the defendant, developed some arguments which may appeal to his Parliamentary colleagues, but will not, I fear, enhance his reputation at the Bar.

Sir Anthony Slatt, Q.C.: Milord, with great respect . . .

The Lord Chief Justice: Quiet, Sir Anthony.

He contended that the £1,500 was not 'profit and

gains' but an 'allowance' towards the expenses of a legis-
lator. If that were so the whole sum would be free of
income tax. But, in fact, where a Member has other
sources of income the Parliamentary 'pay' is lumped
with them for purposes of income tax and surtax and, in
fact, in many cases he enjoys the use of very little of it.
The Court does not, as a rule, concern itself with the
speeches of Members of Parliament: but here we take
judicial notice of the fact that in a recent speech the
Chancellor of the Exchequer referred more than once to
the Member's 'salary'. So that cock must withdraw from
the arena.

Then Sir Anthony said that membership of the House
of Commons could not be described as an 'office'. In my
opinion it can, for, according to the *Oxford English Dic-
tionary*, an office means: 'A position or place to which
certain duties are attached, especially one of a more or
less public character; a position of trust, authority, or
service under constituted authority; a place in the ad-
ministration of government, the public service, etc.'

The Attorney-General argued then that if the defendant held an 'office of profit' he could not be said to hold
it from the Crown. He is not in the employ of Ministers;
indeed he belongs to the Opposition: and the money was
voted by the House of Commons, in the name of the
people. Yes, but it was the Crown, that is, the Ministers,
who made the proposal. The Members may carry resolu-
tions till they are tired: but without the deliberate initiative of the Crown these payments could never have been
authorized or made. Technically, therefore, there is an
opening for some of the very suspicions which prompted
Section 25 of the Act of Queen Anne. Mr. Wilpot and
his friends may not be employed by the Crown, but they
are beholden to the Crown. For all the elector knows

there may have been some improper agreement or men-
ace. The defendant and his friends may have undertaken
not to oppose some Government measure, if this increase
of salary were moved by the Ministers—they may have
threatened to obstruct the Government business if it were
upheld.

There is no evidence of any such thing: but that matters not at all. In most cases, in this honourable land, it
will be found upon examination that such precautions
were unnecessary: but that is not to say that they ought
not to be scrupulously observed. Whatever ingenious
play may be made with words and precedents, Mr.
Attorney, I find that in essence, in the conditions of the
time, the facts are of the same character as our wise ancestors had in mind in 1707. The consequences must be
the same. Mr. Wilpot, and any other Member who has
accepted the increase of salary, whether he voted for it
or not, have vacated their seats, and new writs must issue
for new elections. We are told that this may cause something like a General Election: but that does not concern
the Court. The Members should have thought of that
before.

All the Judges concurred.

31 May 1954

J. B. PRIESTLEY

Student Mobs

BEING A fair-minded man, I begin this piece by admitting that I may have some slight prejudice against students. This is stronger on the negative than on the positive side. It is not that I dislike students as such; it is more that, unlike so many people, remembering their youth, I don't regard student antics through a nostalgic haze. True, I was a student myself once, but then by the time I went up to Cambridge, in the Michaelmas Term of 1919, I was a man not an overgrown boy, already in my twenty-sixth year and a battered old soldier. I wanted to get on with my life and not clown around with lads newly released from school and given their first cheque-books.

I didn't see then—and have never seen since—why young men in universities, turning themselves into mis-chievous and sometimes dangerous mobs, should be treated indulgently, as if they were quite different from mobs of garage hands, apprentice fitters, bus-drivers. Indeed, there is a case for more severity. Students are not supposed to be ignorant and stupid. If they are, then they should be sent home and not receive higher education at public expense. They are wasting not only their own but also other people's time, energy and money. There must be countries now in which peasants are going without substantial meals and some decent clothes so that a lot of lads can spend several years in universities. Such lads should begin to develop a sense of responsibility. They should be the last and not the first to create howling

G   81

destructive mobs. They should be reading books, not burning them.

It is not the occasional 'rags' that get out of hand I am thinking about now; it is the so-called 'demonstrations' that seem to make an appearance every few nights on the TV news. I do not care whose side they are supposed to be on, I am more and more depressed and revolted by these idiot processions, with their banners and slogans and mindless grinning faces, on their way to break windows, smash cars, burn furniture and books, terrify women and children, and to reduce international law, custom and sensible usages to chaos. In many instances, of course, these 'demonstrations' are anything but student improvisations, having been organized by governments on a secret rent-a-mob basis. Even where governments have apologized, it is hard to believe that the student mobs could not have been checked and dispersed before any real damage was done. And this is all part of the darkening picture.

We live in a curious age. We are offered glimpses of a genuine world civilization slowly emerging—the U.N. special agencies, organizations like Oxfam, and here and there, as I have seen for myself, remote enterprises, dedicated to healing or education, with international staffs of selfless enthusiasts. And such glimpses warm the heart and brighten hope. But along with these are sights and sounds that suggest that the whole fabric of civilization, the work of centuries, is rapidly being torn apart. Two official policies clash, and instantly embassies, consulates, centres of information services, are surrounded and then attacked by howling mobs of students, at once defying law, custom, usage. And that this may not be merely so many hot-headed lads escaping all control, that it may itself be part of government policy, mob antics as additional propaganda to deceive world opinion, makes our situation even worse. It is as if we were all compelled to exist now in a sinister circus. No doubt governments have always been dishonest and hypocritical, but now it is beginning to look as if power-mania is ready to destroy those long-accepted forms and civilities that make international relations possible. The time may soon come when ambassadors will have to move around in tanks, and embassies and consulates will have to be fortified or abandoned. And perhaps students on admittance will be given machine-guns and flame-throwers.

There is something else, just as bad, perhaps even worse, and evidence of it is amply supplied to us by TV cameras and mikes. What we see in these student faces illuminated by burning cars and bonfires of books is not the glow of political enthusiasm but a frenzied delight in destruction. Whatever country or party they may be demonstrating for or against, what really inspires them is an urge towards violent demolition. They don't know—and may never know—how to make anything worth having, but they need no courses on wrecking and destroying. If degrees were given in window-smashing, car-overturning, furniture-firing, they would all have them with honours. They may still be weak in sciences and the arts, medicine and the law, but they already have Firsts in Hooliganism. I doubt if some of them even know which side they are shouting for, their minds having abandoned the intricate and tedious arguments of politics as they joyfully contemplate the destruction of other people's property. What sort of doctors and law-yers and chemists and teachers of languages they will make, we cannot tell; but there should be no shortage of recruits with degrees for demolition squads and wrecking crews. Soon there may appear on many a campus those

huge iron balls with which New York keeps knocking
itself down. At a signal from the Ministry of Foreign
Affairs, out they will roll, to demolish an embassy or two
before it is time for any evening seminars.

In this enthusiasm not for politics but for destruction
and violence, these students may be said to be taking their
proper place, right up there in the van, giving a lead to
youth everywhere. For we live, I repeat, in a curious age,
which is trying hard to abolish want and disease but is
also abolishing, without trying, any regard and respect
for other people's possessions. And it is in the countries
where lads are now most carefully and expensively nur-
tured that they proceed to knock hell out of everything.
They may grow up under capitalism or socialism but
what they really care about is vandalism. Now that they
have sufficient money to take special trains to football
matches, they will wreck them on the way back. Well-
paid and full-fed youth has already done more damage
than all the hungry millions of the Bleak Age. Towns
that would not risk a penny rate for the arts are now
having to face a bigger bill every year to restore public
property that has been idiotically or malevolently
destroyed. A woman who had taught in junior schools
for forty years told me that the most recent children
were far and away the most destructive she had ever
known: they just wanted to smash things. It is as if
creatures from other planets had arrived, taking the
shape of playful kids who put things on the lines in the
hope of de-railing expresses.

It was rough in the North when I was a boy there.
Boys came to elementary schools in clogs; on Saturday
nights there were drunken fights, with much smashing
of crockery, in the streets 'back o' t'mill'; and when in
my middle teens I played football (sometimes on grounds

made out of cinder tips) in a local league, both players and spectators could be very rough indeed. But I don't recall any of this curiously malevolent destructiveness and this violence that mark our present time. If youngsters, together with their parents, were aggressively rough, it was because they knew no better, but I cannot remember any of the deeply disturbing psychopathic elements that seems so common today. There might be fights between pugnacious equals but helpless people were not being half-killed merely to round off an evening's amusement. Our destructiveness and violence today do not seem to come from any surplus of energy but from a neurotic or even psychotic heartlessness, a cold disregard of other persons, a hatred of life. And something very much like it, only of course further developed and more subtle, has crept like a huge cold serpent into too much of our fiction and drama. There are people among us who don't seem to belong to the human race. And while I won't join a mob to smash their windows, overturn their cars, burn their furniture and books, I'll be damned if I'll admire 'em.

It is all very odd, bewildering, really rather frightening, for while we can just about deal with it today, what will it be like tomorrow? No sooner do we appear to have made the world safer than a strange half-mad gleam comes into its eyes. The young arrive eager not to create but to destroy. The students never march to build a house but only to knock one down. Like those sinister puffs of steam we notice in New York streets at night, threats of violence, puffing from some hell below, multiply even while we elaborate the techniques and apparatus of a world civilization. And though I am familiar with all the usual explanations—H-bomb, no religion, bad homes and irresponsible parents, dead-end jobs, boring environ-

ment, and the rest—I remain puzzled, never entirely
convinced, still wondering if there might not be some
unknown factor, a vast X in the dark. Meanwhile, I
think I could take some newsreel footage showing me
students making something instead of breaking something—or even just studying.

SIR HERBERT READ

Vulgarity

THE ANTITHESIS of Beauty is Ugliness, but if art, as I have consistently maintained, is a wider concept than beauty, and may even include ugliness, it is only proper to ask what is then art's antithesis. Obviously, I think, it is vulgarity. Vulgarity, as Oscar Wilde said (or ought to have said), is the only sin. The opposite point of view is taken by George Robey, who confessed in his reminiscences (*Looking Back on Life*): 'I believe in honest vulgarity. So did Shakespeare—and if he didn't know what was what nobody on earth ever did. . . . Honest vulgarity is the finest antidote I know to present-day hypocrisy.' So apparently it is not a simple matter; vulgarity is not a merely negative affair. There is honest vulgarity, and there is another kind of vulgarity, presumably dishonest. And honest vulgarity consists in knowing, like Shakespeare, what is what. Perhaps a consideration of the subject from the point of view of the plastic arts will enlighten us.

Vulgarity in its original sense means the taste of the vulgus, the common or uneducated mass of people. But there is good taste and bad taste, and that the taste of the common people is not always bad taste is proved by all kinds of folk-art, which are generally not only in good taste, but in certain periods far superior to the debased products of cultured taste. Vulgarity, therefore, cannot be made a class distinction; it is bad taste in any grade of society, and I doubt if any period of history has been

free from it. But mercifully most vulgar art perishes,
though perhaps there might be something to be said for
preserving specimens of it in some Museum of Horrors,
in which everyone engaged in the production of objects of
use and ornament would be compelled to spend a peni-
tential (or propædeutic) period. Actually such a museum
exists, or did exist, at Stuttgart in Germany; it was only
one section of the Museum, and the choice of objects was
not faultless (there were more appropriate ones in the
other sections of the Museum). But ash-trays in the shape
of water-closets, toilet-rolls printed with patriotic mottoes,
beer-mugs in the shape of Bismarck (or Hindenburg)
were some of the more memorable exhibits.

Inappropriateness is perhaps the basis of our objection
to this kind of vulgarity. Psychologically I think we
should find that the motives behind such types of expression have much in common with the motives behind
laughter. Vulgarity is often desperately serious, but some
of the theories used to explain laughter could be adapted
to vulgarity. Vulgarity is, like humour, a convenient
method of draining off superfluous energy; 'contrast' and
'incongruity' are characteristics of its mode of operation,
and psychological explanations of humour which lay
emphasis on the elements of superiority, contempt or
hostility could find ample support in vulgar objects. That
a sexual tendency is present is shown, not only in the
usual type of music-hall 'vulgar joke', but in many of
the specimens of so-called works of art assembled in the
Stuttgart museum. Perhaps this amounts to no more
than saying that vulgarity is often humorous, but actually
some general psychological theory can be found which
would explain all these departures from human
dignity.

But vulgarity, and the laughter it involves, has its social

value, as Mr. Robey realizes. As he says, it is the finest
antidote to hypocrisy. But that is 'honest' vulgarity, or
shall we say vulgarity justified by the abuses it corrects.
There remains dishonest vulgarity, and I think we shall
find that this is simply vulgarity badly presented. Even
on the music-hall stage, we prefer vulgarity to be expressed by an artist, and a joke made by George Robey is
not quite the same when it is made by someone else. And
though Ruskin thought that this quality had rendered
'some of quite the greatest, wisest, and most moral of
English writers now almost useless for our youth', no one
nowadays would condemn Chaucer or Shakespeare for
their vulgarity. Vulgar they certainly are on occasions,
but with such vigour and artistry that anyone not wholly
inhuman accepts the matter for the sake of the manner.
It is possible that there are certain grades of vulgarity
which no artistry could redeem, but perhaps the ideas
they express could never by any chance enter a sensitive
mind. Most of us are compelled almost daily to wait and
stare at hoardings covered with advertisements, ninety per
cent of which are frankly and even obscenely vulgar; but
if one asks oneself, could a good artist render the same
idea in an acceptable manner, I think in most cases one
has to confess that he could. Why, in spite of that, advertisement agents go out of their way to find artists who are
so excessively crude that they must be quite rare, is one of
the mysteries of the commercial age. Like film producers
and theatrical managers, they must be actuated by false
and fantastic notions of what the public wants. Some of
the larger advertising agencies should be able to test the
matter statistically, but it is not sufficient to compare what
they would call high-brow advertisements with the vulgar
and undoubtedly effective ones. What we need is a comparison of vulgarity well done and vulgarity badly done.

The results might surprise the wiseacres of the advertising world.

We may conclude, then, that vulgarity is synonymous with bad taste, and that it is an affair of the sensibility. We are vulgar, not because of what we say, but because of our manner of saying it. It is a mode of expression, determined by the sensitiveness of our feelings. Whether we wear a loud tie, or speak in a loud voice, or with a bad accent; whether we make rude noises when eating or complete our toilet in public; whether we have cushions of screaming satin (complete with tassels) or receiving-sets in the shape of cathedrals—it is always a failure in sensibility. Whether a fine sensibility is inherited or acquired is another question; but granted a modicum of it, it seems educable. The unfortunate fact is that it rarely accompanies whatever other qualities make for success in the modern world.

ALISTAIR COOKE

It's a Democracy, Isn't It?

I WAS standing on the corner of Lexington Avenue on a Sunday in May waiting for a bus. It was a gorgeous day, hot and golden, and there were not many people around. Sunday is more than a bearable day in New York because for one thing there are about a million less cars than usual. No trucks. Suburbanites in for the day pointing up and down and walking with their feet out. A couple of cabs parked outside a lunch-room, the drivers gone in for a beer. A family or two hand in hand, taking the children off to the park. A well-dressed upper-crust couple coming across from Park Avenue also hand in hand—a very common sight in New York, for Americans are not much concerned in such matters with what looks proper or what the neighbours will think. A good day—the sort of day when, for all the panicky newspaper headlines, your faith in people, and their needs and inclinations, is restored.

Suddenly, I heard a ghost. It was a familiar ghost, an invisible man, somewhere in mid-air saying in a brisk monotone—'Strike. The count is two and two. Runners on first and third.' This lingo, or the language of which this is a snatch, is something you would hear in a hundred places—homes, cafés, saloons, cars—from then till the end of the first week in October. It is a radio sports announcer covering a ball game—a ball game being, as you probably know, a baseball game.

The voice was coming from nowhere. A young Negro

couple, arm in arm, was ambling towards me. But the man's free arm carried a little box. Of course, it was a portable radio. They went down the subway steps, and as they pattered down into the darkness the voice went on floating up, more excited now: 'A base hit to left field. Fuselli's in, Rodgers coming into third.' Nobody else on the street seemed to notice or to care. But if you had cared, and wanted for one day to get away from radio, I don't know where you could have gone. Out at Coney Island, thousands of bodies would be lying in close proximity not only to thousands of other bodies but to hundreds of other little boxes, tuned high. And the air would be so full of 'He's out' and 'The bases are loaded' and 'Full count', that you'd have had quite a time knowing what the wild waves were saying.

This little picture is meant to produce a shudder in you. If it doesn't, then Britons are not what they used to be, and their passion for privacy, and what's more for respecting the next man's privacy, is dead and gone. Don't misunderstand me. I approve myself very strongly of this feeling. I share it. But it makes me all the less of an American. Only a week ago, I heard a plonking sound, allied to music, quite faint, coming up through the living-room floor. It was a neighbour in our apartment house who is either six years of age and a promising pianist or forty years of age and a dope . . . because she—why do I say 'she', I wonder?—has been stuck on that same piece for a month or two now. I grumbled about the sameness of her repertory, and my twelve-year-old daughter, idling over a book, said 'Relax, Pop, you don't have to hear it if you don't want to.'

By this simple remark my daughter didn't mean that I could get up and go downstairs and start a riot, or that I could call the police or take out an injunction. She simply

meant I should shut my mind to the sound. I made sure
this is what she meant, because when I played aloud with
the idea of strangling our tinkling neighbour, she said, 'I
don't think that's very nice. She paid *her* rent too, you
know.'

Now, I should like to say that I am proud of my
daughter and usually turn to her for a response that is
commonsensical and unshocked (by, so far as I can make
out, anything in life). But I wasn't aware she had
acquired so young a fundamental mood or attitude of
what Americans call democracy. In Britain, one of the
minor duties of good citizenship is not to disturb the
private life of other citizens. In this country, it's the
other way around—not to disturb other citizens who are
enjoying their private life in public. That, as you see, is a
heavily loaded interpretation of an attitude that is universal among Americans. And there are limits. Just the
same, the decision of a Washington court of appeal not to
let advertisers broadcast in public buses only shows how
far you can go in America without being stopped.

Americans regard most of us born in Britain as dull,
decent, amiable people but given to being rather testy
about our rights. So 'Relax, Pop,' says my daughter and
goes back to reading her book with one third of her mind,
listening to the pianist downstairs with another lobe, and
at the same time dreaming on all cylinders about some
absent male of the species. Quite aside from the principle
involved, this attitude entails a considerable physical
feat. It is the ability not to hear what you don't want to
hear, what the most famous radio critic in America calls
'selective deafness'. He says it is a faculty essential to an
enjoyment of American radio, and it is a faculty that most
visiting Britons would rather not develop. Because they
soon learn, as Mr. Crosby—John, not Bing—remarks, that

the advertising people are aware of this conditioned reflex and so from year to year, like drug addicts, they increase the dose of the sales talk they cut into the programmes. Still, nobody hearing his favourite comedian or forum discussion or symphony concert bothers to turn off the 'plug'. He lets it chatter on about some soap that 'atomizes dirt' or a tooth-paste that is 'kind to gums but murder on film'. And then, the ecstatic announcer stops, and so back to Bob Hope or 'Whither Europe?' or the second symphony of Beethoven.

To watch an American on the beach, or crowding into a subway, or buying a theatre ticket, or sitting at home with his radio on, tells you something about one aspect of the American character: the capacity to withstand a great deal of outside interference, so to speak; a willing accept-ance of frenzy which, though it's never self-conscious, amounts to a willingness to let other people have and assert their own lively, and even offensive, character. They are a tough race in this. You are expected—far beyond what other peoples would say were the restraints of manners—to assume that one man's opinion is as good as another's. The expert is an American idol, but only in certain understood fields. He is safe from contradiction if his expertness is in a science—in medicine, technology, industrial research, or in making something with his hands (better, if he uses somebody else's hands, because that shows he has mastered a process which can be left to drones): such things as an automobile, a waterproof watch or a non-riding girdle. But when it comes to ideas about life and love and religion and education and archi-tecture and painting and music, indeed all forms of pleasure, there is a national conviction that an expert is a phoney, or 'wants to be different', and that what matters is you should know what you like and—this is a democracy, isn't it?—speak up and say your piece. It may well be born from generations of living close to many races and many prejudices and temperaments and having to strike a liveable compromise that may not be as smooth as some other societies; but at least it is a society, a going concern, which had to be built not out of a theory but out of the urgent practical need to get along at all.

At any rate, if you want to live here in any spiritual comfort you have to allow for a wide variety of temperament in your friends and neighbours and approve a sharp clash of tastes. An insistence on privacy in such a society looks, as it would not look in Britain, like a form of conceit or neurosis, a refusal to admit the status quo by which you all live. So if the issue ever came up in argument, I think most Americans would say that it is merely elementary good manners and good citizenship to look on yourself as only one member of the community whether that community is a town, a party, or a family.

It may be what makes Americans so easy-going about their children. I don't know if anyone has ever taken a statistical count, and there may be just as many nagging parents here as anywhere else, but my impression is that if you are what they used to call a severe disciplinarian with children, you get known to the neighbours as a crank. There is a sort of cheerful, unstated assumption that children will grow up and be polite soon enough and that there's no sense for the first fifteen years or so in pretending they are anything but inhabitants of the jungle. (There is a certain family pride in seeing your child become king or queen of the jungle.) The children themselves are of course not aware of being particularly bad or violent or ill-mannered. They have no other system to compare themselves with, and like all children don't even know that any other system exists. Remembering this, you can appreciate that if a six or a ten or a fifteen-year-old passing you on the street, looks up and says, 'Hi!' he is paying you far more the respect of a genuine liking than if he said, 'Good morning, sir'—which would be a very alien, not to say sarcastic, sound in these parts.

The same sort of tolerance explains too, I think, such a seemingly irrelevant thing as the variety of men's clothes in a big city. There is not among Americans anything remotely resembling the uniform of the English city businessman. They dress for themselves, with their own tastes in ties, shirts, shoes; and this gives to an American street a colour, often a garishness, and it makes it pretty impossible for a foreigner to guess at the occupation of the other men around. With women, it is even more difficult. A flock of girls comes into a restaurant and you can't tell the débutante from the shop girl. I remember a Swedish girl on a ski-ing party watching the swirl of people in the snow and saying, 'Which are the nice people? Who are my kind? Give me a sign.' There are signs. But they are small and subtle and would take her years to learn. And if she stayed here long, she would insensibly shed the signs she sought.

I was taking an Englishman the other night up to my apartment, and as we approached the entrance of the apartment house, I saw a man who lives in the building polishing the radiator of his car. I hissed to call my friend's attention to him as we came close. 'Tell me quick,' I said, 'what sort of an American is this—I mean is he a banker, a real-estate agent, a baseball player or what?—look him over.' My friend leered politely at him sideways. He was a middle-aged dark man, with a black moustache and big eyes. He was hatless. He had on a blue sports coat, slacks of a different colour, a button-down collar and a bright tie. He was polishing away and coughing smoke all over the radiator. Then he bent down to start on the wheels. Standing genially over him was the janitor, saying the utterly meaningless sentence, as we came on it: 'No, sir, not for my money . . . but some guys are that crazy, I reckon.' When we got inside I looked at my friend.

'Oh, I don't know,' he said, 'I should say an advertising man or perhaps the owner of a chain of drug stores.'

'That,' I said, as we went into the lift, 'is a dethroned Archduke.'

He was dethroned by the bullet that shot his great-uncle and started the First World War.

H

PAUL JENNINGS

The Case of the 1,251 Beards

THERE IS a faint but ineradicable feeling of silliness about the act of shaving. Man wakes from sleep and nothingness to life and identity, but before he can move about, making his confident statements to the universe, he must, every morning, go through this curious static dance, mopping and mowing to his reflection in the mirror, half ghost and half hairy animal. (I often cut my ear, but this is probably exceptional.) No one really knows what to think about while shaving.

But I know, now. I think, endlessly, about The 1,251 Men. I have been buying a certain kind of shaving cream for years, and I have only just noticed that it says on the carton it 'has been proved in actual tests by 1,251 men, to make beards easier to cut, to give SMOOTHER, MORE COMFORTABLE SHAVES to three men out of four'.

This claim seems to me to have a gentle, wandering vagueness exactly in tune with the consciousness of a man while shaving. It starts off so confidently (*proved, in actual tests*) and ends on such a mild shoulder-shrugging note, admitting that one in four—roughly 313 of these 1,251 men—gruffly denied having had a more comfortable shave, that one warms to the manufacturers straight away.

If one tries to imagine this test carried out in the usual way, with casual interviews or house-to-house calls, one soon runs into difficulties. One sees the market research boys drawing up a list of eighteen subtle questions ('1. Why do you shave?'); they prepare 1,251 little cards with slots for age-group, profession, income, and even sex (although of course the survey is only of men). They send out their most experienced interviewers. But these neat academic plans are soon upset by the untidy realities of life. At nearly all the houses called on the man, of course, is out at work. If he is at home it is usually an unshaven tough in vest and trousers who growls ' 'op off, mate. I only shave Sat'dys.'

They try calling before breakfast, when the man *is* shaving, but the children crowd in, round-eyed, the cards become smeared with marmalade. They finally abandon the house-to-house method when their 403rd subject, a waspish little man who has entered 'Professor of Logic' against Profession on his card, snaps 'Yes, yes, I quite see the need for some kind of empirical verification. But kindly define your terms. Smoother and more comfortable than what? Than other shaving creams? Than an electric razor? Than *pumice stone*? And have you standardized the hardness of the water?'

No, surely the whole thing was at once more genial and more controlled. One sees all these 1,251 men being tested simultaneously, at some special function. It would be perfectly ethical to choose a place where the water is soft; and this in England means the north-west, away from chalk and limestone formations. On a summer Saturday two special trains, one from London and one from the Midlands, pull into the station of a pretty little Lake District town. These trains are full of bearded men. A huge marquee has been set up in a verdant park, between the grey stone houses and the sweeping hills. A fleet of coaches takes the bearded men to it.

First they are entertained to lunch, there are welcome

speeches and photographs, a band plays musical-comedy selections on a stage decorated with hydrangeas. Then the tests begin; fifty men at a time, at a row of special wash-basins. But although officials in white coats with arm-bands saying TESTER scurry about like sheepdogs, there is something in the atmosphere, half-way between a flower show and an Army reunion, that makes it happily impossible to co-ordinate things.

The public address system crackles with announce-ments: 'If your card shows Test Number Five will you please report to the basins NOW': but they are only half heard above the laughter at the bar, where beer bottles and crumpled cardboard plates lie on the trampled grass. Knots of laughing men, with that extraordinary air of having known each other all their lives that will be familiar to anyone who has ever joined the Army with a large intake, gather in the canvassy twilight; occasionally a summer breeze slaps the walls of the marquee against the poles; bursts of applause can be heard from an im-promptu cricket match that has developed outside.

Some of the bearded men are already in the middle distance, walking along the path by the clear tumbling river with local girls. Others, watching their cronies actually doing the tests at the wash-basins, encourage them with cries of 'Hack it off, Ginger!' And some of them, observing the chinless, naked effect produced, have second thoughts about undergoing the test at all.

For whatever reason, in the end only three out of four men give positive results. But somehow the genial makers don't seem to mind. Nor do I.

KEVIN FITZGERALD

Death of the Business Letter

THERE WAS a time when, if you wanted something from a business house which you thought had got it, you wrote as follows:

Dear Sirs,

I have seen your advertisement for wooden sheds in this week's *More and Happier Gardening*. Have you anything which might fit into an awkward corner, eleven by thirteen, which I have on a southern slope by the rhododendrons in my little garden? It is pleasant to see the crocuses, is it not?

Very truly yours,

KEVIN FITZGERALD

By return of post you got a reply from 'Rustic Sheds and Grottoes Limited' which read something like this:

Dear Sir,

Thank you for yours. Our 'Potters Delight' Shed, number eight in the enclosed leaflet, might just go into that corner of yours if we adjust the doors to open inward which we shall be pleased to do. You are luckier than us, our crocuses are seldom out as early as this but at least we have them to look forward to.

Very truly yours,

Rustic Sheds and Grottoes Limited,

HARRY BLENKINSOP

Manager.

After consideration you replied:

Dear Mr. Blenkinsop,

Thank you for your letter. Yes, I've had another look at the site and your number eight 'Potters Delight' shed will just fit. It is good of you to suggest making the door to open inward because this makes the whole thing possible. Please send me your number eight shed for which I enclose my cheque. May I take it that full directions for putting the thing up in my garden will come with it. My Kaufmannia tulips are a comfort in these chilly days.

> Very truly yours

After about a week you got—in those happy, happy days—your final letter from 'Rustic Sheds and Grottoes Limited'. It went like this:

Dear Mr. FitzGerald,

Thank you for your order and cheque. We have to-day handed your number eight 'Potters Delight' shed to our carriers and it should be with you in the course of a few days. You will find full assembly instructions nailed to the inside of the door component kit, but if you have the slightest difficulty, please get in touch with us. No, our tulips have been a disappointment this year.

> Yours very truly,
>
> HARRY BLENKINSOP
> Manager.

Now take the situation today. You see an advertisement for, say, draught-proofing windows and you write as follows:

The Manager,
The 'Gales-in-the-House-Prevention' Company, Tud-
dington-in-the-Green
Dear Sir,
    I have seen your advertisement in this month's
Rickety Homes about draught-proofing material. In
this cottage I have only casement windows. Will your
material do for such? Have you a stockist anywhere
near here or do I deal with you direct?
                    Very truly yours

After a week you get a letter from the 'Gales-in-the-
House-Prevention' Company. It is stencilled on blotting
paper and it reads as follows:

Dear Sir, or Madam, or Occupier,
    In response to your inquiry we enclose a leaflet.
                    Yours faithfully

There is no signature and no date. Despite a feeling of
disappointment, you open and read the leaflet. There is
no mention anywhere of casement windows and no
reference to the kind of place where you might find the
draught-proofing material. There is a curious phrase at
the bottom of page two: 'Trade terms on application
from bona fide builders' suppliers', and there is something else. The whole document has obviously been written by someone who has spent his entire life fitting
draught-proofing material to windows. This is the kind
of English prose employed:

    Fixing demands a simple Ganymede back thrust
    deployment gouge gauge, size seventeen on the Ber-
    nire or twenty-three by Harrisons Mondellic jig block.
    All that is then needed is a twist with a binding jewel-
    rigged otier screw-plug adjuster.

You think I am exaggerating? I am in fact under-stating. For this is the point. Practically no one now-adays in any big organization is allowed to write a letter. All that can happen is that the nearest form, or circular, to the kind of inquiry you are making is selected by someone unfamiliar either with your problem or its solution, and if you are lucky this is sent to your correct address.

If you doubt this, let me give you a first-hand example. I wrote asking for particulars about investing in a company which makes much in its advertisements of being the largest of its kind in the world. In reply I received a booklet which answered no single one of my questions and which, to me, was in addition completely unin-telligible. It may be that I have a pretty dull mind, but if I ask specific financial questions of a financial house I certainly do not want them answered by a general leaflet composed by their actuary or some economics graduate: what I want is information in words of one syllable set out by someone like me who did not know the answers until he ran about the place finding them out. The people who write the leaflets and booklets I am getting these days (and, I repeat, they send no letter with their stuff), know far too much. We, the recipients, are ignorant chaps and we do not want a copy of Battlecock's 'Expecta-tion of Life in Samoa' chart when we have written to find out if we are still young enough to buy a little insurance.

Of course, most of our difficulties are due to office planners, method study men, and the economy maniacs. In order to save one chap dictating to one girl a pleasant informative letter to a paying customer like me, or you, vast machines are installed with rows of extra people to operate them. Scores of planners are engaged in getting answers out of high-speed machines which put all the decimals in the wrong places every time there is a power cut. And eventually girl 117 gets FitzGerald's letter of inquiry about a garden shed three weeks after it has been written. On it, by the time she gets it, are inscriptions. They read as follows:

Inscription One
Have we dealt with this man before? Try Credit control. H. Blenkinsop, Timber Revetting Manager.
Inscription Two
This is not for us. Z. Jenkins, Coal Export Department.
Inscription Three
Had you better not deal with this, Harry? It's nearly a fortnight old. Is this man a shareholder?
Inscription Four
Betty, Mary says you know the leaflet he wants. Do you dear? Ursula.
Inscription Five
No dear. He sounds rather a fuddy-duddy, doesn't he? Try Millicent in Telephones, Betty.
Inscription Six
Received in Accounts in error. This is for Liverpool I think. Should not someone acknowledge?
Inscription Seven
This is a literature request. Get the man something from Booklet Store, Ramsgate.

Booklet Store, Ramsgate, is where girl 117 works. When she at last gets my letter and has read all the inscriptions I have listed, she goes and looks long and searchingly at rows and rows of booklets in pigeon-holes. If I am lucky, I will get a leaflet or booklet having something to do with my inquiry. If I am only fairly lucky, I will receive a gigantic envelope containing the entire history of the firm, a copy of the chairman's report for 1961, and a brochure describing the new factory at Tuddington-on-the-Green. But if girl 117 is fed up with me, her boy, and life in general, I shall get a printed post-card saying 'Thank you for your communication which is receiving attention'. That, as we all know, is the end of the matter for everyone.

My theory to explain all this, which I have not much exaggerated, is that the captains of industry, the leaders of business, the great bankers, the whole establishment of tycoonery, are not only afraid of the written word but are unable to control it. Put one of these men at a telephone with a couple of charts in front of him and a slide rule within reach and he is the master. Ask him a question in writing and he's done. There is actually nowadays no method of dealing with a letter which requires the sort of reply which might indicate creative thinking somewhere. Such a reply would have to be drafted by Jack and initialled by Mack. Then a committee would sit upon it and a fresh draft would go up to the board. It would be enough to end the correspondence at birth for one thick-headed but important member of the board to say 'There are dangers in discussing that point, I feel, chairman.'

As he returns to his office the chairman says to his number eleven secretary, 'That FitzGerald letter, Margaret. We've decided not to answer his inquiry. Get his girl'—that's what they say—'Get his girl on the telephone and say we're not in a position to handle the matter.' He never knows that FitzGerald has no girl (such a man cannot exist in the minds of chairmen) and really only wanted to know the price of a shed, but was foolish enough to include some personal reflections in his letter.

Let me finish with an absolutely true story and then you will see that the business letter is, alas, completely dead and, I fear, with no chance of revival.

Many years ago the head of a department in which I worked said to me 'What a pity it is, Kevin, that old Blank owes us so much money. It isn't as though he couldn't pay, it's just that he won't. He's such a nice chap and we should hate to put him into the legal department for the recovery of the money. Anyhow, Kevin, try him once more. Write today and ask him please to settle our account.'

So I did. I had met old Mr. Blank several times when he had come in to place business with us, and I wrote telling him exactly the position. I said:

Dear Mr. Blank,

The head of this department has just finished telling me what a pity he thinks it is that you won't settle our account. He says that you have plenty of money, and that he will hate putting our legal department on to your affairs. I don't think it can be very pleasant to have that sort of reputation around this office and I am sure, now that you know what is being said and is going on, that you will let me have your cheque. Bis dat qui cito dat, and all that.

Yours sincerely,

KEVIN FITZGERALD

By return of post, yes, by return of post, Mr. Blank sent his cheque in full. He also said that my letter had made him laugh, that he would give us more of his business now that he knew that we knew what he was like, and he finished up:

It must cheer up your customers if you write to them all like that.

But mark what happened to me. I was sent for by a director, no less, and reprimanded. When he had finished, I said: 'But sir, before I wrote you hadn't got the money and had little hope of getting it without suing Blank. As a result of my letter you have the whole of your money and Mr. Blank has said that he enjoyed the transaction and will give us more of his business.'

And what do you suppose that director said? He said: 'Never mind all that, FitzGerald, we can't have people like Blank getting letters from people like you. That sort of thing creates the impression that we employ poets, and that would never do. It wouldn't be businesslike.'

So the business letter about business is dead. And instead of it we have the trade circular about nothing. I regret this and I keep doing my best to revive the old and honourable practice. And in the recent long months of cold weather it paid me handsomely. My coal merchant much preferred, he said, my description of an 'iced-up wife' to the peremptory demands which flooded his office. He answered my letter the same day—and with bags of coal.

PENELOPE MORTIMER

Apart, Not Together

A FEW years ago a certain American magazine discovered that the world is a revolving sphere and that everything in the place goes round and round. This discovery, as I shall try to explain, led to the first philosophical concept ever to show a financial profit—'Togetherness'. The connexion may not seem immediately clear: but wait.

The world is round. It is not a rectangle; it is not a circular disc, placidly floating in celestial vapours. If it were, people would fall off the entire time. It would be a precarious, nerve-racking existence—jockeying for position, nothing to hold on to, kicking your neighbour savagely in the shins and listening to his screams of despair as he fell like a stone, or watching his smug smile as he ascended, like a gas balloon, into the upper regions.

But—the world is round. Therefore the fact that a human being is roughly constructed in a straight line, never to merge with other straight lines until a remote (and in any case chancy) infinity, was seen to be illogical. The design, they said, is not functional. It is not conforming with nature. It doesn't get anywhere; at least, not fast enough. It must have been at this point that some spry member of the editorial staff recalled—one can imagine his modest pride—the original circular man-woman described by Aristophanes. Each of these creatures, according to Aristophanes, was globular in shape, with four arms and four legs, and two faces, both the same, on a cylindrical neck. When they ran they simply whirled round and round; and they bowled along, apparently, at a pretty good speed. This was exactly what the founders of Togetherness, some twenty-four centuries later, had in mind. In future, they said, the individual must roll around like a hoop. In future, ends must meet, corners be knocked off, heads and heels be grafted together in perfect harmony.

With the aid of tranquillizers, hypnosis, and the cunning promotion of relaxation as an enviable virtue, this globular human being was not hard to perfect. The majority of such creatures, when subjected to gentle warmth and a persuasive pressure, were found to be remarkably pliable. Next, however, came the problem of their relationships to each other.

There was a rather crude, rough and ready design for this already in existence. It was called the Family Circle: an idea perfectly proper in shape, but unworkable now, since it required a pivot, formerly supplied by an old-fashioned man; or—as he was sometimes called in this context—prop, support, or mainstay. It was necessary, therefore, to design a new-type family circle which would be both strong and flexible enough to contain two or more exactly similar human units, and at the same time to find some dynamic that would not only keep the whole contrivance together but actually weld the separate individuals and make them, in time, an intrinsic and indistinguishable part of the whole.

This force, of course, was empathy. Empathy is a kind of deep-ray method of thought, a series of emotional television sets by which it is possible to acquaint oneself, at any time or in any place, with the most lurking thoughts, moods, fluctuations of feeling in the person or people with whom one is Together. It is most easily practised, naturally enough, in an atmosphere where there *are* no

thoughts, moods, or fluctuations of feeling. Togetherness set out to achieve such an atmosphere.

First, rather obviously, solitude had to be made impossible. The old-fashioned house, with its separate rooms
for sleeping, eating, sitting, drawing, cooking, breakfast,
morning, dressing, and even occasionally guns, must go.
In a honeycomb of sound-proof walls Togetherness would
never catch on. Open-plan living was the remedy—a
system of areas contained within four, frequently glass,
walls, and divided, where absolutely necessary, by natural
vegetation. Furniture, which had previously been constructed in separate entities—lonely tables, isolated chairs,
solitary, unhappy broom cupboards—sprang together and
became unified: long, unbroken surfaces sinking nearer
and nearer to the floor in a passionate longing for homo-
geneity. And the floor itself, of course, was carpeted from
wall to wall: no more of those desperate little rugs, no
more egomaniacs triumphantly keeping their feet warm
on private islands of Axminster.

By this time it was clear that Togetherness was no idle
dream, but a way of life; and that this way of life needed
a considerable income. It was therefore necessary, in view
of the dangers inherent in its title, for Togetherness to
make itself socially clear.

A Togetherer may only get together with his own kind.
A Togetherer must accept the fact that outside the magic
circle there are a distressing number of 'squares'—the
poor, the wild, the unsuccessful; the blind, the irresolute,
and the fool who hopes; the careless, the slap-happy; the
child who plays by himself and the old man who waits by
himself; the madmen, and all those who have no grade
to make, no bus to catch, no benefit to reap. By disassoci-
ating itself from all social obligation or responsibility,
Togetherness overcame the pitfalls of logic and was free

to direct itself towards a simple but magnificent purpose
—the improvement of the middle classes, the idealization
of goods. Togetherness became, in fact, the philosophy
of boom.

Let us, for a moment, see what it means. The human
unit glides on its prescribed daily course, round and
round, through the areas of its barely necessary chores.
The hum of machinery hardly stirs the rubber plant, and
the light is dim. Surrender; submerge; relax. All those
loose ends, snags and jags, bits and pieces that used to
clutter your soul are smoothed away. You will never be
alone again. Husband and wife, gently illuminated with
pride, hover over the washing-up machine; husband and
wife empathetically joined, flow out of the family car
and seep like ectoplasm into the living area where their
children are engaged in the corporate passivity of watching television. Together—as far as hygiene and the curiously old-fashioned medical profession would permit—
they gave birth to these children. Their faces glow with
resolute goodwill towards themselves. So excellent is the
family breakfast food, so habitual their orgies of milk,
that they are almost the same size. Their clothes are the
same, their tastes are the same; their hopes, abilities, experience, and dreams are all entirely the same. Joined, in-
separable, unanimous and uniform, they drop away and
are left alone only in death : and quite suddenly the lights
go out, the wind blows cold, they are naked souls swirl-
ing like leaves in the dark. The whole fatuous lie has
exploded into nightmare.

Togetherness, which started as a journalist's gimmick,
has become the bland justification of materialism and
conformity. It sends us racing in ever-decreasing circles.
Its subliminal promise is love, understanding, and progress : it provides only a receipt to prove that once again

I

we have done better than the Joneses. We are led to expect the glow of comradeship, the final breakthrough into social awareness—and we get a soft drink, twopence back on the bottle. We are encouraged to hope that at last some tender benefactor may give us what we deserve for being so good, so loyal, so hard-working, so corporately gay—and we are offered some form of confectionery or soap, sweets for the soul and detergents to remove the stains of guilt. We earnestly attempt empathy and only manage to tune in to some nasty broodings, better left alone. Small wonder that Togetherness has led to dizziness, apathy, and the inability to distinguish between emotional indigestion and heart-failure.

So if we must—and in this day and unsafe age it seems necessary—have a notion, something fancy, expensive, and only remotely connected with human needs, to encourage us, what can we turn to now? The obvious answer is that we should break the vicious circle and revive the idea of a beginning and an end. Perhaps we can only be more merrily together if we have perfected the technique of being severely, even ruthlessly, apart.

Spread out. Build walls, follies, summer houses, bothies. Set up, where necessary, wigwams. Our homes, far from being open or planned, should be microcosms of life—that is, they should be complex containers for a variety of eccentric tastes: small plaster gnomes, large marble monuments, Picasso and Foxhunter, Jacobean and Japanese, freedom for pin-ups and privacy for tears. How can you beat your head against a brick wall when there isn't one? How, come to that, can you read, write, pray, practice standing on your head or playing the trombone other than in total solitude? The ideal is for every member of the human race to have a door of its own to lock fast.

An impossible ideal, I grant you—and its implications, like those of Togetherness, are far from cheery. One must assume that the desire to shut a door is followed, in due course and in the normally integrated and enlightened person, by a desire to open it. Although one cannot, of course, guarantee the reappearance of mystics, saints, or hermits—or those who out of pure absentmindedness happen to have lost their key.

The fact remains that agreement is only valuable when it is the result of independent thought; that progress is only possible by the voluntary association of a number of individuals—who have come, not to an end in their thinking, but to a conclusion. What we need is far more solitude, an immeasurably great degree of apartness—in each one of us a private wilderness in which, if only for forty winks, we can contemplate the fact that there may quite possibly be a hundred billion thumbs in this world, each one of them with a different imprint. For every man to say, like Gibbon, that he is never less alone than when by himself—this, surely is the essence of wisdom and the inspiration for a new campaign based on respect and dignity. I offer it, at a cut-rate to first-comers, to all those who feel they can further exploit a human need—to be solitary, to be curious; and to be left alone.

ANONYMOUS

Put that Seaweed Back

ONE OF the inherent benefits in the British way of life
is that Britain has no written constitution. The lives of
citizens of other countries are well regulated and preserved by declarations, articles, dependent clauses and
amendments. Tidy, but a little dull. Life in Britain can
hardly ever be dull so long as we have judges who, in
response to public demand, are willing from time to
time to engage in bouts of historical criticism. One of the
unexpected bonuses that the public obtained this week
from the civil division of the Court of Appeal was the
declaration that (in law) no clear decision could be found
that the public had any right to walk on the foreshore
when the tide was out.

Our only clear right, apparently, is the right to pass
over the foreshore in boats, for the purpose of fishing,
when the tide is in. Bathing is tolerated, but only just.
Riding, driving, gathering seaweed—these are not rights
but activities licensed by the Crown. In short, as one of
the three learned judges put it, it is notorious that many
things are done on the sea shore by the public which they
have no legal right to do.

The Court was, of course, settling a serious point. This
exegesis was provoked by a case in which a group of
people had been removing sea coal from a stretch of the
Durham coastline on a commercial basis, to the annoy-
ance of the Easington Rural District Council and a
merchant who had been licensed to do the same thing.

The Court finally held that the first lot of sea-coal gatherers had no right to be there.

Well and good, but can the matter rest there? What are our citizens to think, and how are they to behave, when next summer they head for the beaches of the United Kingdom? There is little reason to expect a sudden upsurge in the incidence of sea-coal gathering, unless it comes as a result of British determination to reassert what used to be regarded as an immemorial right.

This, it has to be said, is a pretty small risk. We have got to like this business of being governed. So, all for the sake of sea coal, local authorities have been reminded that they have some residual powers which they had more or less forgotten about. It would come as no surprise to see fresh crops of official notices sprouting along our shores next year—'Bathing Tolerated', 'Donkey Rides Licensed Here', 'Seaweed Gathering Permitted', 'Walkers Must Have an Approved Licence', 'Sitting Allowed from 8 a.m. to 7 p.m.'

MARGARET LANE

The Boyhood of Fabre

GENIUS SEEMS rarely to break out spontaneously, with nothing to account for it. There is generally some predilection, however slight, in family or environment, some traceable influence or happy chance to breathe on the spark and feed the first smouldering mental ardour which will blaze in maturity. The great composer is born in a family of musicians, or one that at least has had some contact with music; the poet, even Burns at the plough, is touched, as by the tip of a finger, by education; and there is a tradition of scientific inquiry in most of the families which have produced great scientists.

Yet once in a way the miracle seems to occur; an effect of great splendour is produced without visible cause. There will be a sort of immaculate conception, and a mind of great power and originality will develop where heredity and environment would lead one least to expect it, engendering in itself, apparently without any fertilizing contact, a violent impulse towards some science, some art, which it pursues with unaccountable love.

This seems indeed to have been the case with Fabre, who all his life was puzzled by the contrast between what he was born and what he had become. The question appears and reappears in varying forms all through his *Souvenirs Entomologiques*, massive and beautiful harvest of his scientific life. How did it start? Where did it come from, this passionate interest in the grasshopper, the

wasp? He was never able to find the clue, and neither
can we. The fascinating puzzle remains: a child of
ancient poverty, ignorance, prejudice, superstition, forc-
ing himself, unaided, and as though beckoned by a vision,
into the clear exhilarating light of scientific discovery, to
become the observer, the interpreter, the poet of a hidden
world.

Jean-Henri Fabre died in 1915. It is with a start that
one realizes he was born in 1823, the year when Dickens
was pasting labels in the blacking warehouse; the year
Byron sailed for Greece.

He was the child of illiterate and poverty-stricken
peasants who were always trying, and always failing, to
scrape a living off the barren stony uplands of the
Cevennes. ('One of the most beggarly countries in the
world,' said Stevenson, when half a century later he
travelled it with a donkey, 'like the worst of the Scottish
Highlands, only worse.') Snow, wind and wolves were
their enemies in winter, and in summer the limestone
plateau dried and bleached like a skeleton. Almost nothing would grow.

To be rid of one hungry mouth, Fabre *père* sent the
boy in infancy to live with his grandparents, and it is
with another inward start that one grasps his description
of these survivors from the eighteenth century. Both were
totally illiterate, and knew of the world beyond their
own granite plateau only by hearsay. His grandmother
still wore the huge eccentric head-dress of the Rouergue;
his grandfather was a typical sour and silent peasant of
the *ancien régime*.

I always remember his serious look; his unshorn locks,
often thrust with a fist behind one ear and spreading
their antique Gallic mane over his shoulders. I see his

small three-cornered hat, his short breeches buckled at the knee, his resounding wooden sabots crammed with straw.

To them, cattle were interesting as a means of livelihood, and the wolf as a dangerous neighbour; but beyond these the brute creation was ignored. An insect, lower still, was something to be washed out of a cabbage with a grunt of disgust or cracked under a thumb-nail. Yet it was from the hearth of these grandparents that Fabre, a barefoot urchin, wandered out into the heather to satisfy his first absorbing curiosities—the beginnings of that passion for personal knowledge of phenomena which was soon to develop his genius for exact, intimate, and yet imaginative observation. He has left us a curiously touching account of his first scientific experiment, conducted when he was five or six years old:

There, in solitude, among geese and calves and sheep, I awoke to the first glimmerings of intellect. Behold me one day, hands behind my back, a dreamy urchin, gazing at the sun. This dazzling splendour fascinates me. I am a moth, drawn to the light of the lamp. Is it with my mouth or with my eyes that I apprehend this glory? Such is the question posed by my dawning scientific curiosity. Reader, do not smile: the future observer is already practising, experimenting. I open my mouth as wide as possible and close my eyes. The glory vanishes. I open my eyes and close my mouth. The glory reappears. I begin again. The same result. Now it is done—I know for a fact that I see the sun with my eyes.

The special marks which so richly distinguish Fabre from other naturalists were already perceptible in the boy, if anyone had been interested. He was by temperament and imagination a poet, and it was from nature and especially from the beautiful, grotesque, unknown and almost inscrutable world of the insect that he received his most intense aesthetic experience. He saw, with an imaginative grasp rare indeed in that peasant environment, that the world was by no means only man's. The insect creation—blind and indifferent to man as man to the insect—was more varied, complicated, bizarre, following patterns of marvellous ingenuity and skill which were all the more startling because, clearly, instinct and not intelligence was at work. It was, in some ways, a nightmare world; yet it had a compelling beauty. In it the female was entirely dominant and terrible—huntress, devourer, mighty mother, allowing the inoffensive drone, the small and anxious male spider to exist only to perform his necessary but despised function. Sometimes his necessity, even, was all but ignored: among the mantises the male was often carelessly devoured during copulation, while among certain pond and plant flies whole generations were produced and reared without sexual contact. (Were these strange formulae of reproduction, Fabre came to wonder, relics of earlier experiments on the part of the Almighty, before, in the higher creation, He hit on the reproductive plan which apparently satisfied Him?)

To the ragged child, now going daily to sit on a back bench in the schoolmaster's earth-floored cottage, the beauties of the despised insect world spoke with the force of revelation. He finds a beetle, 'smaller than a cherry-stone, but of an unutterable blue', and carries home his 'living jewel' in an empty snail-shell, plugged with a green leaf. The image of a pigeon, roughly printed on the cover of the ABC, invites him more kindly than the letters which no one can be bothered to explain.

His round eye, ringed with a coronet of dots, seems to smile at me. His wing, of which I count the feathers one by one, speaks to me of soaring flight among the lovely clouds; it transports me to beech woods, their smooth trunks rising from a carpet of moss where snowy mushrooms peep, like eggs deposited there by some wandering fowl; it carries me to snowy summits where my bird leaves the starry imprint of his rosy feet.

Later, through the miserable boredoms of a squalid school, he consoles himself under the shelter of his desk, examining a snapdragon berry, a wasp's sting, the wing-case of a beetle, an oleander fruit.

Fabre himself, though in the *Souvenirs* he returns again and again to the fringe of the question, was never able to determine at what point in his dreaming boy-hood it became clear to him that what he wanted was *knowledge*. From that unidentified moment, however, it was the sole end to which he struggled, against what difficulties, hardships, discouragements, he alone fully knew. His parents, worn down and embittered by pov-erty, saw no necessity, once he could read and write, for further schooling. Only by the hard way of scholarships and self-support could he prove his claim to a grudging continuance of education, and even this was interrupted for long periods as his parents, who had failed first as far-mers, and then as keepers of a succession of sordid little village cafés, claimed his labour, and he was sent to work as a stone-breaker on the railway, or the roads, or to stand selling a handful of lemons on the corner of the street.

Yet through these discouragements, marvellously, his resolution hardened, and from his letters to his younger brother, whom he dragged after him up the steep path of education, we feel something of the almost mystic experience which the unfolding of the intellect, and the apprehension of his own faculties, had become.

Today is Thursday; nothing beckons you out of doors; you choose a quiet corner where only a soft light penetrates. There you are, elbows on table, a fist behind each ear and a book before you. Intelligence awakens, will-power takes control, the external world dissolves, the ear no longer hears nor does the eye see, the body is no more present; it is the soul that studies; she remembers, she summons up her learning, and light is born. Then the hours fly away, quickly, quickly, so quickly, there is no counting the time. Is it already evening? . . . But a flock of truths is ranged together in the memory, difficulties that delayed you yesterday have melted on reflection, whole volumes have been devoured, and you are content with your day.

Perhaps it was as well, for posterity, that he had no very clear idea of where this learning was leading him. Faith and reason both told him that it would lead to independence, to that path of science towards which his imagination ardently pointed, to freedom to work his own rich vein of scientific ore. And so, for his last thirty years, from the time Fabre was sixty until he was close on ninety, it certainly did. But the preceding forty years, the whole prime of his life, were to be worn away by poverty and the struggle for existence; by ceaseless striving to support a growing family on a primary-school teacher's pittance; by hack-work, producing countless little school text-books—jewels of lucidity indeed, but very far from being the life's work to which he now knew himself committed. If he could have foreseen those forty years of frustration, ever working to earn the means to buy leisure to work, never quite achieving it, he might have renounced the struggle, and we should have been without the *Souvenirs*, marvellous fruit of his last years of observation and reflection, haunted by memories of his boyhood as by a recurring dream.

One thinks of Darwin (with whom, in old age, he corresponded eagerly to disagree) and his long life of research made possible by domestic peace and private means. 'I have had ample leisure,' Darwin wrote in his autobiography, 'from not having to earn my own bread.' One remembers the moneyed and cultured background, Shrewsbury, Cambridge, the heaven-sent opportunity of the five-year voyage in the *Beagle* . . . and the great evolutionist, the charming and lovable recluse of Down, is not difficult to explain.

What a contrast to the hopeless beginnings, the discouragements, the lack of recognition, the bitter poverty of Fabre! There is something exquisitely painful in the thought that he was sixty years old, and white-haired, before he had scraped together sufficient savings to retire behind his garden wall at Sérignan and embrace the work of his life.

The contrast between the recluse of Down and the recluse of Sérignan is painfully clear; but peace descends on liberated genius at last, and behind the high Provençal wall, for thirty years, the great work is being written. Letters are passing, too, between the two old men, mutually arguing, contradicting, acknowledging one another. The fact that Fabre, in old age, learned English the more freely to communicate with Darwin (with whom he disagreed), seems to gather up, as into the palm of one's hand, all that is most touchingly patient, noble, even religious, in the scientific spirit.

J. H. PLUMB

Josiah Wedgwood

JOSIAH WEDGWOOD was a pioneer of the Industrial Revolution. For many of us who were bred in the liberal tradition, such a phrase conjures up a picture of a square-jawed, steely-eyed grinder of the faces of the poor. You might expect him to be a man of inflexible character, narrow, philistine and possibly hypocritical: one whose interests were limited to profit and the accumulation of capital: and, perhaps, indifferent to poverty, squalor and human suffering: one of those men whose sole memorials are the mean streets of the dirty towns which erupt like boils across the Midland plain. Naturally there were such men—every rapid social change creates an opportunity for the tough and the heartless—but Josiah Wedgwood was not one of them. Certainly he was tough. You have only to look at the Reynolds portrait of him to realize that. His jaw was formidably square, almost brutal. And only a tough-minded man could have done some of the things that Wedgwood did for the sake of his business. He had a weak leg, the result of a serious illness in childhood: the slightest knock caused inflammation and pain, and knocks were unavoidable when riding through the deep muddy Midland lanes in winter. So to avoid the long periods of sickness and the interruption of business Wedgwood had the leg amputated. In those days there were no anaesthetics, no sterilization of instruments; each act of surgery was a gamble with death. The key to much of Wedgwood's success in life was his boldness and courage in decisions such as this. Although Wedgwood's square jaw immediately attracts the eye, no one can look at his picture without realizing that he was far from being a simple man. His eyes are wide, frank, inquiring, but his mouth perhaps is even more interesting than his eyes. It is soft, sensual, the one beautiful feature of that powerful, ugly face. The final impression of this portrait is of strength, intelligence and, oddly enough, compassion— a quality not often associated with a pioneer of industrial revolution but one borne out by the story of Wedgwood's life.

He was born in 1730 at Burslem—then the only 'town' in the Potteries and not a very prosperous one at that. His family was typical of a curiously English mixture of class. He was descended from a long line of small land-owners; some had married well, others had drifted into trade, most eked out their inheritance with a small pot-tery business. But it was a family of wide connexions and one which possessed a number of useful reserves of capi-tal. Wedgwood tapped one of these when he married his cousin, Sarah, the daughter and heiress of a prosperous cheese factor in Cheshire. The origins of many of the great figures of the Industrial Revolution were similar to Wedgwood's. Few of them were born in absolute poverty; most of them came from families with a little money and a knowledge of trade.

As potters the Wedgwoods were well known and quite successful within the narrow limits of the Staffordshire trade. The invention of salt glaze in the 1690s and the proximity of the great Cheshire salt deposits gave the district a fillip in the early years of the eighteenth century. By the time, however, Wedgwood was growing to man-hood in the late 1740s, the industry was losing ground. The *naïveté* of much of the salt glaze was beginning to bore the public. The gentry and aristocracy preferred Dutch pottery or German porcelain, or the even more costly porcelain imported at great cost from China. The English products were too heavy, too grossly decorated, too obviously peasant ware for the growing refinement of the wealthy classes.

The potters knew it and Wedgwood grew up in an atmosphere of experiment. From his earliest days he was determined to improve Staffordshire pottery. He was a man of enormous patience and resource and once set on a course, not easily deterred by failure. That square, obstinate chin was highly symbolic of his rugged determination. Before he perfected his famous Jasper ware—that blue or sage-green pottery with white decoration which immediately springs to the mind when Wedgwood is mentioned—he made over ten thousand trial pieces. From the first he set his standards very high and that was one of the reasons for his success. He tried and finally succeeded in making English pottery almost as fine as the best that Europe or China could offer. I say 'almost as fine' deliberately. It was never Wedgwood's intention to produce a few exquisite masterpieces. From the start he wanted to capture a world market; to make fine pottery cheap enough for the middle classes and beautiful enough for kings and princes. That is why from the first he concentrated his attention on his 'useful' pottery, the white Queen's ware which quickly achieved an international reputation; Catherine of Russia ordered a magnificent dinner service of a thousand pieces; a generation later a service followed Napoleon to St. Helena. In the years between, the use of Wedgwood had spread to the uttermost ends of the earth.

This astonishing achievement which poured a new invigorating wealth into the Midland counties was not

easily brought about. Great difficulties needed to be over-
come; and technical advance was not enough by itself.
For one thing the human material was not very tractable.
The Staffordshire potters were no more easy to discipline
than most eighteenth-century craftsmen who liked doing
their jobs in their own way and in their own time. They
wandered from process to process as the mood seized
them; worked hard and then drank hard. Everything
was done by fits and starts. That was not Wedgwood's
way, and once they started to work for him those habits
had to change. In his factories hours were regular and
processes methodical, so that production could be continuous. Exhortation, rewards, punishments and education—by these methods Wedgwood created a factory
system capable of mass production of fine quality pottery.
At the same time, he provided far more stable and profit-
able working conditions than the journeyman potters had
ever known. Increased trade and population increased
amenities—schools, musical festivals, literary and scientific institutes—all were encouraged by Wedgwood. They
helped to dispel the medieval barbarity into which so
many of the potters had been born. Living conditions improved greatly. It is hard for us to realize that. The mean,
crumbling slums which we view with so much disgust
represented in the eighteenth and early nineteenth centuries a triumph in working-class conditions, an advance
on the mud and wattle rural slums of the earlier centuries.

Disciplined labour, systematic production, high technical achievement, even these were not enough to secure
Wedgwood's success. In his early youth, coal for firing
the potter's oven had frequently to be carried on the backs
of men—no other beast of burden could struggle through
the deep quagmires which the roads became in winter.
Packhorses and the wagons of summer time were not

K

much cheaper than men. The raw materials, salt, lead-ore, coal and the fine clays from Dorset, Devon and Corn-wall, were all bulky, all expensive to move. Hence it is natural to find Wedgwood in the forefront of the battle for improved communications, and here luck was on his side. Liverpool, under the energetic inspiration of a small band of highly intelligent merchants, was growing fast. The Duke of Bridgewater and his engineer Brindley were beginning to solve some of the problems which its growth created by developing artificial waterways or canals. Liverpool was the natural port for Staffordshire and Wedgwood became the leading agitator for a Trent-Mersey canal which, however, involved far more diffi-cult engineering problems than any previously tackled by Brindley. Of course there was much opposition but the tide of life was with Wedgwood and his friends. They got their canal and were splendidly justified—freight was reduced from 10d. to 1¼d. per ton per mile.

It needed, however, more than efficiency and cheap transport to capture a mass market; more even than fine technique. Wedgwood had to win and keep the approval of the fashionable world. During one of his visits to Liverpool Wedgwood was laid up for many weeks with that leg of his. He was introduced to a Liverpool mer-chant, Thomas Bentley. They became devoted friends and lifelong partners. Bentley was a highly sophisticated and sensitive man with a wide knowledge of art, well known and respected in the literary and scientific circles of London. He brought Wedgwood into contact with ideas and attitudes which stimulated his imagination. It was through Bentley that Wedgwood obtained the ser-vices of Flaxman, one of the finest modellers of his day. Bentley conducted the firm's London showrooms with great skill and such profit that Wedgwood was able to indulge both his love of experiment and his ambition to repeat, if not surpass, the ceramic triumphs of the ancient world.

By middle age Wedgwood had transformed a peasant craft into an industry with a world market, yet one whose products were acclaimed as works of art by informed opinion. Now Wedgwood believed that his success was due to scientific experiment, to the steady application of rational principles to all problems, and to riding rough-shod over traditional attitudes and ancient prejudices. 'All things,' he wrote, 'yield to experiment.' Naturally, there-fore, he was drawn to the society of men whose views on life were similar to his own; to men such as Priestley, Darwin, Franklin and their kind, men who believed in applying reason to the problems of politics and society. Bentley held similar views, and the two partners became stalwart supporters of that admirable liberal humanism of the late eighteenth century. They believed in parlia-mentary reform and universal suffrage. They denounced the slave trade; one of their finest cameos was of a slave kneeling in chains with the inscription: 'Am I not a man and a brother?' Wedgwood told Bentley that he blessed his stars and Lord North that America was free from the iron hand of tyranny. He refused to be scared into obscurantism by the spectre of the French Revolution. In spite of the loss of trade, he welcomed it. Wedgwood believed passionately that he and his friends were the harbingers of a new and better world from which pre-judice and poverty would be banished and in which rea-son would triumph. A naïve attitude, perhaps, but one which mirrors the noble aspects of eighteenth-century life. His beliefs were very much of his time and place, as was his success, yet not entirely so. He possessed compassion and the ebullient, life-giving quality of genius. He would never prosecute a debtor; rich as he became he loathed accounts and ignored them; he paid no attention to the little men who pirated his works.

> So far from being afraid of other people getting our patterns, [he wrote to Bentley] we should glory in it. . . . There is nothing relating to business I so much wish for as being released from . . . those mean selfish fears of other people copying my works.

In that fine, expressive face which mirrored so accurately his complex nature, it was the fine eyes and sensitive mouth which in final analysis dominated the rugged jaw. In the largeness of his heart and the liberality of his mind he transcended the age in which he lived.

The seeds of creative genius settle and flower in curious places. In the fertile mind and active personality of Josiah Wedgwood they found good soil. Amongst the arts and crafts that adorn the life of man, his works still have an enduring place, and remain unmistakably his. His personality, his individual genius, make them as singular as a Dickens novel or a Bach fugue. Eighteenth-century England bred few men of finer quality.

CHRISTINE ORTON

A Queen of Music

LILY PAVEY was working as a copy-typist for a cable
firm when she got her idea. 'I was sitting at my typewriter thinking if only I'd taken that job with a music
publisher I'd have been typing about music all day instead of bloomin' telegrams. Typing music—that's a good
idea, I thought. Smashing. Typewriters type words. Why
shouldn't they type music?'

That was fifteen years ago and it has taken all the time
in between to invent and perfect her machine and finally
have it accepted. Now the Pavey Musigraph is on sale.
With just forty-six keys it can copy any kind of musical
score, a feat which no one, apart from Miss Pavey her-
self, ever thought possible.

Meet Miss Pavey and most of one's preconceived notions
about egg-head inventors disappear pretty quickly.

She is young-looking, brown-haired, aged forty-eight
and lives in a council flat. There was no mistaking which
flat when we had climbed to the third floor in South
London's Bermondsey. Outside the front door, waiting to
be carted off with some other rubbish, was a dilapidated
typewriter and several screwed up sheets of musical score.

Inside the flat was Miss Pavey, four feet nine small,
slightly Cockney and bright as a Pearly Queen's button.
She bursts with warmth and welcome. Her words pop
out of her mouth just as she thinks them, a perpetual
bubbling flow with a schoolboy's penchant for blimey
and smashing.

In one corner of her small sitting-room stands an electric organ which, cups of tea and chocolate biscuits distributed, she promptly sits down at and starts to play. Shades of the cinema invade the room.

A quick look round takes in flowery curtains and net at the windows, plastic-topped sideboard and matching table. Three clocks, all exactly half an hour fast, tick away in frantic rivalry. On the floor sits twelve-year-old son John fondling pet hamsters.

'Music sends me,' said Lily Pavey, playing on. A Bach toccata jostled with Gershwin's *Rhapsody in Blue* on the music stand. 'As long as it's good of its kind I love it all. In my show business days they called me "Queen of the Music".'

Lily Pavey was brought up in a circus, she told us, settling down now among the yellow taffeta cushions on her settee. Her mother was a dancer, her father a clown 'complete with baggy pants, red nose and all'. At four Lily joined in, too, dancing in the ring between acts with a different dress for each dance.

At twelve she had an act of her own, playing a variety of musical instruments—violin, piccolo, trumpet, guitar.

Life was so busy she really had no time to fit in education—musical or otherwise. 'Pity, because I always fancied a cap and gown,' said Lily wistfully. Although self-taught, her grasp of some of the finer technicalities of orchestration and musical score, let alone the Musigraph, is quite extraordinary.

Talk to Lily Pavey long and one's more conventional ideas about life turn upside down. The impossible suddenly seems possible, the incredible perfectly credible. Take the Voice, for instance.

'I'll tell you something very surprising,' she says seriously. 'When I was a child I had a dream in which this

Voice—Father I call him—told me I would do something very special when I grew up. Something that others had tried but failed in.'

Just what, Lily didn't know. 'I certainly didn't imagine inventing anything though I suppose you could call me the inventive type. I like to work things out for myself, taking no notice of what he says, what she says, what I've read somewhere.'

Patiently she waited. At nineteen she married, but her husband was killed in the war leaving her with her eldest son Raymond. She married a second time, sold her musical instruments to make a home and took up copy-typing when the marriage broke up. Then, when she was thirty-three, came her idea.

'After the first enthusiasm I told myself not to be so daft. First, I knew nothing about typewriters. Secondly, I hadn't any money. "Shut up," I thought. "Get on with your typing." And then, do you know, I heard the Voice, telling me not to be a defeatist.'

She took notice and dashed out to patent her idea, paying for it with six guineas borrowed from her boss. ' "Blimey, you're determined," he said.'

Determined Lily was. First she bought a secondhand typewriter ('It had to be British. I'm very patriotic') and studied the mechanism. Amazingly it did not take her long to master the secret which had baffled others. She discovered a way to give the machine vertical elevation over a wide area so that notes could be placed at any point on the stave without the paper moving.

She made her first prototype with bits of wood and string and started the rounds of typewriter manufacturers. It took a long time to convince anyone that she was not just another crazy crank.

'There's nothing so mad as a not yet successful inventor,' reflected Lily, 'though I believe I was considered less potty than some.'

It was a tough time. She had to live on National Assistance and sold all her furniture to buy new patents but she persevered. Why? 'Because of faith and the Voice.'

Miss Pavey has no other interests; all her friends are fellow members of the Institute of Inventors. Now she's working on a new device to be used in teaching music. She knows this time people will listen.

'Not that I minded that much when they didn't,' she told us. 'Like that Kipling chap said: "If you can meet with triumph and disaster and treat those two impostors just the same . . ." well, you're all right.'

ROBERT GRAVES
The Poet and his Public[1]

HERE I sit, alone in a sound-proof room, at a table bare
but for my papers, a pencil, and a glass of water. I am
supposed to be addressing my public, as members of other
professions in this series have addressed theirs. An awkward situation. The chances are that not more than one
person in every hundred has read my poems even by
mistake—except perhaps a few rhymes which I wrote
nearly forty years ago and which have got fossilized in
school anthologies. The chances are equally against any
immediate increase in the number of my readers because
of this broadcast.

The B.B.C., you will notice, have not supplied me with
an audience to make encouraging noises and laugh in the
right places, as they do for highly-paid comedians. I dare
say they might have raked together a sympathetic audience, if I had insisted. (I was an old friend of the Cor-
poration's while it was still only a Company and an-
nounced itself as 2 LO; when you veteran listeners were
using home-made crystal sets with cat's whiskers; and
every time a bus went down the Strand you heard the
rumble.) But a poet needs no audience: he can do very
well without the giggle or horse-laugh so necessary for
the comedian. The comedian tries to make his public as
large as possible, and loses no opportunity of meeting it
in person; he takes it out to dinner (so to speak) and pets
it, and gives it photographs signed in enormous round

[1] A Home Service broadcast.

handwriting—'To my own darling Public, from your adorer Charlie'. And he joins in every merry romp that will bind him and it more lovingly together. The poet behaves quite differently towards his public—unless he is not really a poet but a disguised comedian, or preacher, or space-buyer.

Frankly, honest Public, I am not professionally concerned with you, and expect nothing from you. Please give me no bouquets, and I will give you no signed photographs. That does not mean that I am altogether untouched by your kindness and sympathy, or that I dislike the money which two or three thousand of you invest in new volumes of my poems. All I mean is that these poems are not addressed directly to you in the sense that the comedian's jokes are; though I don't in the least mind your reading them. Of course, I also write historical novels, which is how I make a living. My motive or excuse is usually to clear up some historical problem which has puzzled me, but I never forget that these novels have to support me and my large family. So I think of the average, intelligent, educated general reader, and try to hold his attention by writing as clearly and simply and unboringly as the subject allows. Money's tight these days, and I should think very ill of myself unless I made the novels as lively as possible—just as the greengrocer or butcher prides himself on selling the freshest, tastiest produce of the market, and at a reasonable price. Here duty and self-interest go hand in hand; because once one tries to pass off bad stuff as good, the customer will shop elsewhere and advise his friends to do the same.

Towards my poetry-reading public, however, I feel no such tenderness. By this I do not mean that I have stricter standards in prose than in poetry. On the contrary, poems are infinitely more difficult to write than prose, and my standards are correspondingly higher. If I re-write a line of prose five times, I re-write a line of verse fifteen times. The fact is that I could never say: 'Funds are low, I must write a dozen poems.' But I might well say: 'Funds are low, it's time I wrote another novel.' Novels are in the public domain, poems are not. I can make this last point clear by talking about important letters. Most of the important letters you write fall into two different categories. The first is the business letter—'Sir: I beg to advise you in reply to your communication of the 5th ultimo . . .'—written with an eye on office files. This sort of letter is in the public domain. But not the other sort, the personal letter beginning: 'Darling Mavis, when we kissed good-bye last night . . .' Or: 'Dear Captain Dingbat, you go to blazes!'—in each case written to convey a clear and passionate message, and without a thought for any libel suit, or breach of promise action, in which it may one day be produced as evidence against you. So with poems. We must distinguish those written with a careful eye to the public files from those written in private emotion. Of course, this comparison is not quite exact. Though some poems (for example, most of Shakespeare's *Sonnets*) are in the love-letter category, and others (for example, a couple of the same *Sonnets*) are in the 'You go to blazes!' category; yet in most cases the poet seems to be talking to himself, not either to his beloved or to his enemy.

Well, then, for whom does he write poems if not for a particular Mavis or Captain Dingbat? Don't think me fanciful when I say that he writes them for the Muse. 'The Muse' has become a popular joke. 'Ha, ha, my boy!' exclaims Dr. Whackem, the schoolmaster, when he finds a rude rhyme chalked on the blackboard. 'So you have been *wooing the Muse*, have you? Take that, and that, and that!' But the Muse was once a powerful goddess. Poets worshipped her with as much awe as smiths felt for their god Vulcan; or soldiers for their god Mars. I grant that, by the time of Homer, the ancient cult of the Muse had been supplanted by the cult of the upstart Apollo, who claimed to be the god of poets. Nevertheless, both Homer's *Iliad* and Homer's *Odyssey* begin with a formal invocation to the Muse. When I say that a poet writes his poems for the Muse, I mean simply that he treats poetry with a single-minded devotion which may be called religious, and that he allows no other activity in which he takes part, whether concerned with his liveli-hood or with his social duties, to interfere with it. This has been my own rule since I was fourteen or fifteen, and has become second nature to me.

Poems should not be written, like novels, to entertain or instruct the public; or the less poems they. The path-ology of poetic composition is no secret. A poet finds him-self caught in some baffling emotional problem, which is of such urgency that it sends him into a sort of trance. And in this trance his mind works, with astonishing boldness and precision, on several imaginative levels at once. The poem is either a practical answer to his prob-lem, or else it is a clear statement of it; and a problem clearly stated is halfway to solution. Some poets are more plagued than others with emotional problems, and more conscientious in working out the poems which arise from them—that is to say more attentive in their service to the Muse.

Poems have been compared to pearls. Pearls are the natural reaction of the oyster to some irritating piece of grit which has worked its way in between its valves; the grit gets smoothed over with layers of mother-of-pearl until it ceases to be a nuisance to the oyster. Poems have also been compared to honey. And the worker-bee is driven by some inner restlessness to gather and store honey all summer long, until its wings are quite worn out, from pure devotion to the queen. Both bee and oyster, indeed, take so much trouble over their work that one finds geography books saying: 'The oysters of Tinnevelly yield the most beautiful pearls on the Indian market,' or: 'The bees of Hymettus produce the sweetest honey in the world'. From this it is only a step to the ridiculous assumption that the oyster is mainly concerned in satisfying the Bombay pearl merchants' love of beauty; and the bees delighting gourmets at the world's most expensive restaurants. The same assumption, almost equally ridiculous, is made about poets.

Though we know that Shakespeare circulated a few of his less personal sonnets among his friends, he is unlikely to have had any intention of publishing the remainder. It seems that a bookseller-publisher, one Thorp, bought the manuscript from the mysterious Mr. W. H., to whom they were addressed, and pirated the whole series. Nevertheless, a poem is seldom so personal that a small group of the poet's contemporaries cannot understand it; and if it has been written with the appropriate care—by which I mean that the problem troubling him is stated as truly and economically and detachedly as possible—they are likely to admire the result. The poem might even supply the answer to a pressing problem of their own, because the poet is a human being, and so are they. And since he works out his own problems in the language which they happen to share, there is a somewhat closer sympathy between his public and himself, even though he does not write directly for it, than between the oyster and the oyster's public, or the bee and the bee's public.

A poet's public consists of those who happen to be close enough to him, in education and environment and imaginative vision, to be able to catch both the overtones and the undertones of his poetic statements. And unless he despises his fellow-men, he will not deny them the pleasure of reading what he has written while inspired by the Muse, once it has served his purpose of self-information.

Young poets tend to be either ambitious, or anxious to keep up with fashion. Both these failings—failings only where poetry is concerned, because they are advantages in the business world and in most of the professions— encourage him to have designs on the public. The attempt to keep up with fashion will lead him to borrow the style of whatever poet is most highly approved at the time. . . . Now, I have known three generations of John Smiths. The type breeds true. John Smith II and III went to the same school, university and learned profession as John Smith I. Yet John Smith I wrote pseudo-Swinburne; John Smith II wrote pseudo-Brooke; and John Smith III is now writing pseudo-Eliot. But unless John Smith can write John Smith, however unfashionable the result, why does he bother to write at all? Surely one Swinburne, one Brooke, or one Eliot are enough in any age?

Ambition has even worse results. The young poet will try to be original; he will begin to experiment: a great mistake. It is true that if an unusually difficult problem forces a poet into a poetic trance, he may find himself not only making personal variations on accepted verse forms but perhaps (as Shakespeare and Hardy did) coining new words. Yet innovation in this sense is not experiment. Experimental research is all very well for a scientist. He carries out a series of routine experiments in the proper- ties (say) of some obscure metallic compound, and publishes the results in a scientific journal. But poetry cannot be called a science; science works on a calm intellectual level, with proper safeguards against imaginative freedom.

And what is all this nonsense about poetry not paying? Why should it pay? Especially when it is experimental in the scientific sense? Poets today complain far too much about the economic situation, and even expect the State to support them. What social function have they? They are neither scientists, nor entertainers, nor philosophers, nor preachers. Are they then 'unacknowledged legislators' as Shelley suggested? But how can unacknowledged legislators be publicly supported by the legislature itself? If a poet is obsessed by the Muse and privileged to satisfy her demands when he records his obsessions in poetry, this in itself should be sufficient reward. I doubt whether he should even bargain with the public, like Wee MacGregor (wasn't it?) with his school-friend: 'Gie me a bite of your apple, and I'll show you my sair thumb!' It always surprises me to find that my personal poems have a public at all; probably most of my readers buy them because of my novels—which I think is a very poor reason.

So much for the poet in his unjustified search for a public. Now about the public in its justified search for a poet. Public, you sent me a one-man delegation the other day in the person of a worthy, well-educated, intelligent, puzzled paterfamilias, who happened to be closely connected with the publishing trade. This is how he began: 'I must be getting old and stupid, Robert, but I can't really follow more than an occasional line of this modern poetry. I feel quite ashamed of myself in the presence of my boy Michael and his friends.'

I asked him to explain. 'Well,' he said, 'when I was

young and keen on modern painting I had a fight with my father because he couldn't appreciate Toulouse-Lautrec or the Douanier Rousseau. And now an important Toulouse-Lautrec fetches as much as a Botticelli; and if you own a Douanier Rousseau, you have to install a burglar alarm. . . . Michael and his friends take the same line about Mr. X and Mr. Y; and so does everyone else at Cambridge. Mr. X's *Collected Poems* have recently sold ten thousand copies, and Mr. Y is regarded as the highest apple on the tree. *All* the critics can't be wrong.'

'Why can't all the critics be wrong?' I asked. 'If you mean the un-poets who set the Paris fashions. Who decides on this year's skirt-length? Not the women themselves, but one or two clever man-milliners in the Rue de la Paix. Similar man-milliners control the fashions in poetry. There will always be a skirt-length. . . . And as William Blake said: "In a Commercial Nation impostors are abroad in every profession." How do you know that twenty years hence Messrs. X and Y won't be as old-look as Humbert Wolfe and John Freeman, who were public idols twenty or thirty years ago?'

He said: 'Toulouse-Lautrec and Rousseau aren't old-look.'

I pacified him by agreeing that it would take a lot to kill either; or, for that matter, Botticelli. Then he asked the question that you are all itching to ask me: 'How can you tell good poetry from bad?'

I answered: 'How does one tell good fish from bad? Surely by the smell? Use your nose.'

He said: 'Yes, perhaps with practice one can tell the clumsy from the accomplished. But what about the real and the artificial?'

'Real fish will smell real, and artificial fish will have no smell at all.'

He thought this rather too slick for an answer, so I explained: 'If you prefer the painting metaphor, very well. The test of a painting is not what it looks like in an exhibition frame on varnishing day; but whether it can hang on the wall of your dining-room a year or two after you bought it without going dead on you. The test of a poem is whether you can re-read it with excitement three years after the critics tell you it's a masterpiece. Well, the skirt-length of fashion has wandered up and down the leg from heel to knee since I first read my elder contemporaries Thomas Hardy and William Davies and Robert Frost; and my younger contemporaries Laura Riding, Norman Cameron and James Reeves. They have all at times written below their best, and none of them are in fashion now, but their best does not go dead on the wall.'

To conclude. The only demands that a poet can make from his public are that they treat him with consideration, and expect nothing from him; and do not make a public figure of him—but rather, if they please, a secret friend. And may I take this opportunity for appealing to young poets: not to send me their poems for my opinion? If they are true poems, they will know this themselves and not need me to say so; and if they are not, why bother to send them?

L

GEORGE ORWELL

Why I Write

FROM A very early age, perhaps the age of five or six, I knew that when I grew up I should be a writer. Between the ages of about seventeen and twenty-four I tried to abandon this idea, but I did so with the consciousness that I was outraging my true nature and that sooner or later I should have to settle down and write books.

I was the middle child of three, but there was a gap of five years on either side, and I barely saw my father before I was eight. For this and other reasons I was somewhat lonely, and I soon developed disagreeable mannerisms which made me unpopular throughout my schooldays. I had the lonely child's habit of making up stories and holding conversations with imaginary persons, and I think from the very start my literary ambitions were mixed up with the feeling of being isolated and undervalued. I knew that I had a facility with words and a power of facing unpleasant facts, and I felt that this created a sort of private world in which I could get my own back for my failure in everyday life. Nevertheless the volume of serious—i.e. seriously intended—writing which I produced all through my childhood and boyhood would not amount to half a dozen pages. I wrote my first poem at the age of four or five, my mother taking it down to dictation. I cannot remember anything about it except that it was about a tiger and the tiger had 'chair-like teeth'—a good enough phrase, but I fancy the poem was a plagiarism of Blake's 'Tiger, Tiger'. At eleven, when the war of 1914-18 broke out, I wrote a patriotic poem which was printed in the local newspaper, as was another, two years later, on the death of Kitchener. From time to time, when I was a bit older, I wrote bad and usually unfinished 'nature poems' in the Georgian style. I also, about twice, attempted a short story which was a ghastly failure. That was the total of the would-be serious work that I actually set down on paper during all those years.

However, throughout this time I did in a sense engage in literary activities. To begin with there was the made-to-order stuff which I produced quickly, easily and without much pleasure to myself. Apart from school work, I wrote *vers d'occasion*, semi-comic poems which I could turn out at what now seems to me astonishing speed—at fourteen I wrote a whole rhyming play, in imitation of Aristophanes, in about a week—and helped to edit school magazines, both printed and in manuscript. These magazines were the most pitiful burlesque stuff that you could imagine, and I took far less trouble with them than I now would with the cheapest journalism. But side by side with all this, for fifteen years or more, I was carrying out a literary exercise of a quite different kind: this was the making up of a continuous 'story' about myself, a sort of diary existing only in the mind. I believe this is a common habit of children and adolescents. As a very small child I used to imagine that I was, say, Robin Hood, and picture myself as the hero of thrilling adventures, but quite soon my 'story' ceased to be narcissistic in a crude way and became more and more a mere description of what I was doing and the things I saw. For minutes at a time this kind of thing would be running through my head: 'He pushed the door open and entered the room. A yellow beam of sunlight, filtering through the muslin curtains, slanted on to the table, where a matchbox, half open, lay beside the inkpot. With his right hand in his pocket he moved across to the window. Down in the street a tortoiseshell cat was chasing a dead leaf,' etc., etc. This habit continued till I was about twenty-five, right through my non-literary years. Although I had to search, and did search, for the right words, I seemed to be making this descriptive effort almost against my will, under a kind of compulsion from outside. The 'story' must, I suppose, have reflected the styles of the various writers I admired at different ages, but so far as I remember it always had the same meticulous descriptive quality.

When I was about sixteen I suddenly discovered the joy of mere words, i.e. the sounds and associations of words. The lines from *Paradise Lost*—

> 'So hee with difficulty and labour hard
> Moved on: with difficulty and labour hee,'

which do not now seem to me so very wonderful, sent shivers down my backbone; and the spelling 'hee' for 'he' was an added pleasure. As for the need to describe things, I knew all about it already. So it is clear what kind of books I wanted to write, in so far as I could be said to want to write books at that time. I wanted to write enormous naturalistic novels with unhappy endings, full of detailed descriptions and arresting similes, and also full of purple passages in which words were used partly for the sake of their sound. And in fact my first completed novel, *Burmese Days*, which I wrote when I was thirty but projected much earlier, is rather that kind of book.

I give all this background information because I do not think one can assess a writer's motives without knowing something of his early development. His subject matter will be determined by the age he lives in—at least this is true in tumultuous, revolutionary ages like our own—but before he ever begins to write he will have acquired an emotional attitude from which he will never completely escape. It is his job, no doubt, to discipline his temperament and avoid getting stuck at some immature stage, or in some perverse mood: but if he escapes from his early influences altogether, he will have killed his impulse to write. Putting aside the need to earn a living, I think there are four great motives for writing, at any rate for writing prose. They exist in different degrees in every writer, and in any one writer the proportions will vary from time to time, according to the atmosphere in which he is living. They are:

(1) *Sheer egoism*. Desire to seem clever, to be talked about, to be remembered after death, to get your own back on grown-ups who snubbed you in childhood, etc., etc. It is humbug to pretend that this is not a motive, and a strong one. Writers share this characteristic with scientists, artists, politicians, lawyers, soldiers, successful businessmen—in short, with the whole top crust of humanity. The great mass of human beings are not acutely selfish. After the age of about thirty they abandon individual ambition—in many cases, indeed, they almost abandon the sense of being individuals at all—and live chiefly for others, or are simply smothered under drudgery. But there is also the minority of gifted, wilful people who are determined to live their own lives to the end, and writers belong in this class. Serious writers, I should say, are on the whole more vain and self-centred than journalists, though less interested in money.

(2) *Aesthetic enthusiasm*. Perception of beauty in the external world, or, on the other hand, in words and their

right arrangement. Pleasure in the impact of one sound on another, in the firmness of good prose or the rhythm of a good story. Desire to share an experience which one feels is valuable and ought not to be missed. The aesthetic motive is very feeble in a lot of writers, but even a pamphleteer or a writer of textbooks will have pet words and phrases which appeal to him for non-utilitarian reasons; or he may feel strongly about typography, width of margins, etc. Above the level of a railway guide, no book is quite free from aesthetic considerations.

(3) *Historical impulse.* Desire to see things as they are, to find out true facts and store them up for the use of posterity.

(4) *Political purpose*—using the word 'political' in the widest possible sense. Desire to push the world in a certain direction, to alter other people's idea of the kind of society that they should strive after. Once again, no book is genuinely free from political bias. The opinion that art should have nothing to do with politics is itself a political attitude.

It can be seen how these various impulses must war against one another, and how they must fluctuate from person to person and from time to time. By nature— taking your 'nature' to be the state you have attained when you are first adult—I am a person in whom the first three motives would outweigh the fourth. In a peaceful age I might have written ornate or merely descriptive books, and might have remained almost unaware of my political loyalties. As it is I have been forced into becoming a sort of pamphleteer. First I spent five years in an unsuitable profession (the Indian Imperial Police, in Burma), and then I underwent poverty and the sense of failure. This increased my natural hatred of authority and made me for the first time fully aware of the existence of the working classes, and the job in Burma had given me some understanding of the nature of imperialism: but these experiences were not enough to give me an accurate political orientation. Then came Hitler, the Spanish civil war, etc. By the end of 1935 I had still failed to reach a firm decision. I remember a little poem that I wrote at that date, expressing my dilemma:

A happy vicar I might have been
Two hundred years ago,
To preach upon eternal doom
And watch my walnuts grow;

But born, alas, in an evil time,
I missed that pleasant haven,
For the hair has grown on my upper lip
And the clergy are all clean-shaven.

And later still the times were good,
We were so easy to please,
We rocked our troubled thoughts to sleep
On the bosoms of the trees.

All ignorant we dared to own
The joys we now dissemble;
The greenfinch on the apple bough
Could make my enemies tremble.

But girls' bellies and apricots,
Roach in a shaded stream,
Horses, ducks in flight at dawn,
All these are a dream.

It is forbidden to dream again;
We maim our joys or hide them;
Horses are made of chromium steel
And little fat men shall ride them.

I am the worm who never turned,
The eunuch without a harem;
Between the priest and the commissar
I walk like Eugene Aram;

And the commissar is telling my fortune
While the radio plays,
But the priest has promised an Austin Seven,
For Duggie always pays.

I dreamed I dwelt in marble halls,
And woke to find it true;
I wasn't born for an age like this;
Was Smith? Was Jones? Were you?

The Spanish war and other events in 1936-7 turned the
scale and thereafter I knew where I stood. Every line of
serious work that I have written since 1936 has been
written, directly or indirectly, *against* totalitarianism and
for democratic socialism, as I understand it. It seems to
me nonsense, in a period like our own, to think that one
can avoid writing of such subjects. Everyone writes of
them in one guise or another. It is simply a question of
which side one takes and what approach one follows.
And the more one is conscious of one's political bias, the
more chance one has of acting politically without sacri-
ficing one's aesthetic and intellectual integrity.

What I have most wanted to do throughout the past
ten years is to make political writing into an art. My
starting point is always a feeling of partisanship, a sense
of injustice. When I sit down to write a book, I do not
say to myself, 'I am going to produce a work of art.' I
write it because there is some lie that I want to expose,
some fact to which I want to draw attention, and my
initial concern is to get a hearing. But I could not do the

work of writing a book, or even a long magazine article, if it were not also an aesthetic experience. Anyone who cares to examine my work will see that even when it is downright propaganda it contains much that a full-time politician would consider irrelevant. I am not able, and I do not want, completely to abandon the world-view that I acquired in childhood. So long as I remain alive and well I shall continue to feel strongly about prose style, to love the surface of the earth, and to take a pleasure in solid objects and scraps of useless information. It is no use trying to suppress that side of myself. The job is to reconcile my ingrained likes and dislikes with the essentially public, non-individual activities that this age forces on all of us.

It is not easy. It raises problems of construction and of language, and it raises in a new way the problem of truthfulness. Let me give just one example of the cruder kind of difficulty that arises. My book about the Spanish civil war, *Homage to Catalonia*, is, of course, a frankly political book, but in the main it is written with a certain detachment and regard for form. I did try very hard in it to tell the whole truth without violating my literary instincts. But among other things it contains a long chapter, full of newspaper quotations and the like, defending the Trotskyists who were accused of plotting with Franco. Clearly such a chapter, which after a year or two would lose its interest for any ordinary reader, must ruin the book. A critic whom I respect read me a lecture about it. 'Why did you put in all that stuff?' he said. 'You've turned what might have been a good book into journalism.' What he said was true, but I could not have done otherwise. I happened to know, what very few people in England had been allowed to know, that innocent men were being falsely accused. If I had not been angry about that I should never have written the book.

In one form or another this problem comes up again. The problem of language is subtler and would take too long to discuss. I will only say that of late years I have tried to write less picturesquely and more exactly. In any case I find that by the time you have perfected any style of writing, you have always outgrown it. *Animal Farm* was the first book in which I tried, with full consciousness of what I was doing, to fuse political purpose and artistic purpose into one whole. I have not written a novel for seven years, but I hope to write another fairly soon. It is bound to be a failure, every book is a failure, but I do know with some clarity what kind of book I want to write.

Looking back through the last page or two, I see that I have made it appear as though my motives in writing were wholly public-spirited. I don't want to leave that as the final impression. All writers are vain, selfish and lazy, and at the very bottom of their motives there lies a mystery. Writing a book is a horrible, exhausting struggle, like a long bout of some painful illness. One would never undertake such a thing if one were not driven on by some demon whom one can neither resist nor understand. For all one knows that demon is simply the same instinct that makes a baby squall for attention. And yet it is also true that one can write nothing readable unless one constantly struggles to efface one's own personality. Good prose is like a window pane. I cannot say with certainty which of my motives are the strongest, but I know which of them deserve to be followed. And looking back through my work, I see that it is invariably where I lacked a *political* purpose that I wrote lifeless books and was betrayed into purple passages, sentences without meaning, decorative adjectives and humbug generally.

SIR JOHN SHUCKBURGH

The Birds of St. James's

SOMEBODY (WAS it Mr. E. V. Lucas?) once remarked that St. James's Park always reminded him of Norfolk, because both reminded him of birds. The Park has long been famous for its birds. Water-fowl are said to have been kept there since the days of Queen Elizabeth, but it was at the Restoration that they first became a feature of London life. 'Then to walk in St. James's Parke,' wrote Pepys in August 1661, 'and saw great variety of fowl which I never saw before and so home.' Again, in March 1662, the Diarist spent 'an hour or two in the Parke, which is now very pleasant'; and 'here,' he adds, 'the King and Duke (of York) came to see their fowl play. The Duke took very civil notice of me.'

The King was always coming there. As is well known, 'sauntering' was a favourite amusement of Charles II. It was a relief from cares of State; perhaps even from feminine society, of which that amiable monarch may sometimes have tired. He enjoyed loitering under the trees of St. James's Park and throwing cakes to the water-fowl. He liked to watch their gobbling, just as he liked listening to the debates in the House of Lords. It was all so amusing: almost as good as a play. Perhaps he found the birds better actors than the peers. If they sometimes quarrelled, so did their lordships; and the birds probably made it up sooner and with a better grace. The King's habit, so the historians tell us, made him very popular, for people like to see the great unbend. But he set a fashion which he seems before long to have found embarrassing. Too many people came to the Park: perhaps they saw too much when they got there. At any rate, the nuisance had to be checked. 'I could not get into the Parke,' says Pepys in August 1664, 'and so was fain to stay in the gallery over the gate to look to the passage into the Parke, into which the King hath forbid of late anybody's coming.' A year later he complains that the Park is 'quite locked up'. So Charles had the water-fowl to himself; no doubt they got fewer cakes, but they may have been none the worse for that.

Today there is no Merry Monarch to 'forbid . . . anybody's coming'. The public comes in its thousands, and the birds are fed to repletion. They have grown tame and plump beyond belief. A grey goose will waddle out of the water and rub itself against your leg like a friendly cat. One of the pelicans actually died of the ill-judged attentions of its admirers. These strange creatures have delicate stomachs, and the contents of paper bags do not always agree with them. It has been necessary to put up a notice begging that the survivors may be spared. Londoners are not good at obeying notices. But the appeal on behalf of the pelicans is a *cri de cœur*; let us hope that it will not fall on deaf ears.

St. James's Park, as a bird sanctuary, is probably unique. Is there anywhere else in the world where so many species of wild-fowl can be observed to such advantage, and within so limited a space? The whole collection may be seen in a quarter of an hour. Swan and pelican, peacock and pheasant, cormorant, brent-goose, wild-duck, mallard, coot and dabchick—but what do their names matter? That is the business of the ornithologist, who is welcome to quibble over *genus* and *species* and to revel in Latin polysyllables. Let us watch the pageant and be content.

Keats declared that he did not envy the nightingale its happy lot. Perhaps the soul of our 'sweetest and saddest singer' was so free from earthly littlenesses that he could use the words in all sincerity. But which of us can say the same? In our heart of hearts we all envy the birds. They are our superiors in a thousand ways. After years of effort and frustration we managed to acquire, with the aid of cumbrous machinery, an art which they have practised with effortless mastery since the beginning of time. They are the freemen of the air, we are but blundering intruders into their domain. 'Shadowy race of men, that fall as the leaves fall; poor feeble creatures of clay; wretched wingless mortals, the idle phantoms of a dream.' Such were human beings in the eyes of Aristophanes' bird-chorus. And the birds themselves? Creatures that dwelt in the empyrean, ageless and immortal, and surveyed with pitying eyes the miserable struggles and distractions of the world beneath them.

Does the balance stand otherwise today? We pride ourselves on our civilization, on our social system, on the ordered hierarchy that regulates our lives. Watch the birds; they are as well ordered and governed as we, and they make infinitely less clatter about it. The bird sanctuary in the Park is a State in miniature, a model Republic, in which all classes live together with a reasonable measure of harmony. The three pelicans are the aristocrats of the community. They hold their patent by a title that dates back over two and a half centuries. Evelyn, the Diarist, saw them in the year 1665. 'I went to St. James's Parke,' he says, 'where I saw various animals, and examined the throate of ye *Onocratylus*, or pelican, a fowle betweene a stork and a swan; a melancholy water-fowle brought from Astracan by the Russian Ambassador, it was diverting to see how he would toss up and turn a flat fish, plaise or flounder, to get it right into its gullet at its lower beak, wch being filmy, stretches to a prodigious wideness when it devours a great fish.' To this day the strange creatures have their place apart, as befits their ambassadorial origin. No one molests them, no one intrudes upon their privacy while they perform the solemn, and seemingly unending, ritual of their toilet. And when at length they rise and stalk with conscious dignity down to the water's edge, the smaller fry draw respectfully apart and leave a clear path before them. Once on the water, they pursue their stately course with unruffled serenity: the leader in front, his two followers abreast behind him. The coots and dabchicks scuttle out of their way; it is as if three towering liners were steaming slowly out of harbour through a crowd of small fishing-craft.

Then there are the gulls, a noisy, greedy, restless crowd. They are an alien element in the Cloudcuckooland of St. James's Park. They are not true citizens, but tourists that come only for the winter months. The cold weather drives them in from the sea, as it drives their human counterparts from our Northern mists to the sunshine of Egypt or the Riviera. With the advent of spring they are seen no more. Meanwhile, like others of the tourist class, they know how to make a nuisance of themselves. Their shrill cries and swift rapacity bewilder the slower-moving freshwater fowl. The sober goose is no match for the raucous intruder; duck and mallard look on helplessly as he swoops screaming down and snatches food from their very beaks. For the most part the birds bear patiently with the nuisance. It is the day of the blatant and the grasping, they seem to say. Let them bluster out their little hour, and shriek and pillage to their hearts' content. Such is the normal philosophy of birdland. But there is a limit to the patience of the most acquiescent, both among birds and men. One need not look far afield for illustrations. Events have proved that the endurance even of the long-suffering British nation can sometimes be pushed too far. So too with the denizens of the Park; there are times when they too rally to the common cause against the common enemy. They will endure no more to be robbed of their perquisites; they will show these alien marauders that they are masters in their own house. Their methods on these occasions are simple and effect-ive. They make in solid phalanx for a corner of the lake where the food-distributors are busy on the bank. A cordon of stalwart drakes deploys in semicircular forma-tion—with either flank resting upon the shore—and bids defiance to the invading host. Against this defence the gulls are powerless: behind their living screen the water-fowl deal faithfully with the contents of the paper bags (not without some squabbling among themselves), while the enemy, balked of his plunder but voluble as ever, hovers impotently on the outskirts of the ring. The forces of law and order have asserted themselves.

All this in the day-time, while mankind is looking on. There comes an hour when the Park gates are shut, when darkness descends upon lake and island, and the birds are left to their own devices. Cloudcuckooland is as remote from the world as its ancient prototype; indeed remoter still, for there are no messengers from baffled Olympians to penetrate its ramparts, no idle poet or soothsayer, no villainous informer or parricide, to bring contamination into its sanctuaries. Tereus dispenses justice in his own kingdom, or slumbers in peace beside his nightingale bride. It is pleasant, as we trudge home through the murky London twilight, to think of this

quiet haven in the midst of our crowded streets where
the birds still 'muse on things immortal' and still follow
traditions coeval with the dawn of creation when black-
winged Night laid that first ancestral Egg from which,
as the seasons revolved, Love the Adorable was hatched.

ALISON UTTLEY

Scotties

EVERY DAY my little Scottie tries to escape and wander away to explore the dangerous world of cars and cats and death on the roads. Two old workmen came to my garden to dig a trench for extra wire-netting, to prevent the dog's escape.

'I think animals are blooming well getting too educated nowadays,' said one of the men. 'They understand everything you say. Look at that dog waiting there watching us! He's laughing at us. As soon as we go he'll dig down and tear up the netting and get through.' He grunted and winked at Dirk and then he went on digging.

'We have two cats and they sit listening to the wireless,' he continued. 'When they hear "Fish prices" they get up and walk about. They know the days of the week too. When Saturday comes they know. It is fish day, so they never cry for fish. They wait till afternoon.'

I said to him, 'Do you know the Romans were here 2,000 years ago?'

'Yes,' he replied, rather surprised at my question.

'Do you know that a wall was built across the north country, called "Hadrian's Wall"?'

'Yes,' he replied again.

'Well,' I continued with my history lesson, 'a little bronze figure of a Scottie dog was found there lately and it dates to about A.D. 150.'

'How long ago is that?' he asked.

'About 1,800 years,' I replied. I showed him a picture of the little black dog, a miniature bronze figurine.

'Trying to dig through,' he remarked thoughtfully, and he went on with his own Hadrian's wall.

He was right, the Scottie examined the fence with minute care and thoroughness, moving slowly along it and testing the wire with his sharp teeth. He tugged at it every few inches, and at last was rewarded by a weak place. He strolled away with an innocent air, and bided his time. When he entered the garden the next day he was alone. He went at once to the weak spot and worked hard, until the wire-netting was pulled loose. He got through and escaped, as the man had prophesied. He was just seen as he wriggled under the wire.

He was brought back, an unwilling captive, but he was elated. He wagged his tail, he barked with a little pleasurable cry of joy, he was very proud.

A boy came and mended the hole, and put an extra piece of wire-netting across the weak place. Dirk watched him and made his plans. He could not loosen the wire but he could climb. He went up the netting like a monkey, and when he balanced on the top he gave a squeal of delight mingled with fright, and fell over. He was caught before he escaped, for his cry had betrayed him.

The boy returned and put an extra piece of netting on the summit of the first strip. No dog could climb that, and even a jumper could not get over. Hadrian's wall stood firm at last.

The wall of wire-netting has held firm for six months and the dog gazes through at the passers-by, accepting their homage, a pat, a word of greeting, enjoying the friendship of human beings, but fiercely barking when any stray dog goes this way. He barks furiously and long, to warn off all intruders from his own property.

A Scottie is a fearless little bundle of energy. He is strong for his size, he is often pugnacious, and postmen fear him. This Scottie loves everybody, and the postmen stoop to pat him and talk to him as he lies on the door-step in the morning waiting to welcome them. He rises, wags his upright tail like a flag and bows his head for the touch of the man's hand. One Scottie I had was so fierce he held the postman by the boot, and no work-man dared to go in the house. This little Dirk is gentle, he is loving and giving like a child, for one can take a bone from him or remove his meat with no remonstrance from him. He has had no cross words except when he escapes, and he trusts everybody.

He is much interested in boots, and he looks at my feet to see what I am wearing. A pair of heavy shoes means I am going out, but if I put on these shoes for the garden he leaps round excitedly, trying to persuade me to go for a walk first. He is hard to resist, he has such disarm-ing manners. At the word 'No' he lies in his basket, with head down but eyes fixed on me, ready to spring up in a split second.

In the car he sits with keen enjoyment of everything he sees. He barks furiously at dogs of inferior breed on the pavement, he leaps to the window at the back and tells them what he thinks of them. When I shop he waits patiently, but the window must be nearly closed or he scrambles through. Once I found him standing by the side of a policeman in the midst of the traffic. I could not believe he had squeezed through the tiny window to follow me until he was stopped by the policeman who handed him over to me.

Like a mouse he can flatten himself and get through narrow cracks.

Twice a day he takes me for a walk. For him it is a close exploration of the hedges, as he walks with nose sniffing and head bent, one eye on the lookout for dogs and babies. He adores the very young and we cannot pass a perambulator without a friendly nod to the small inhabitant who nearly falls out as he offers his fingers to the Scottie. Dirk stands on his hind legs to see the baby, he wags his tail, he grins, he shakes his pointed ears, and waves his red tongue in eagerness. A silent talk goes on, between the dumb little dog and the unspeaking baby. Then with waves of hand and tail I separate them and we resume the walk. Little dogs receive a warm welcome, but big dogs are growled at, and barked at and shown that they are inferior beings.

He drags me along and then stops and we contemplate the hedge. My sight is as keen as his and I find simple flowers, the strong-smelling mugwort, the feathery yarrow, the tiny striped pink convolvulus and the white campion. Flowers grow in the hedge shelter, unseen by the people who walk on the pavement, and the little dog and I are contented although we are far from the fields and woods of my youth.

A Scottie is a very wise dog. He understands quickly what is wanted, but he is independent. If it suits him he won't obey. It is too early to go to bed, so he politely remains in the garden, looking at the evening sun, watching the birds, listening to the night sounds. I call, he gives me a glance of recognition, and then he turns back to contemplate until he is ready. He wakes me early, yet not too early. He gives a little bark to call me, and usually I obey, but sometimes I too am disobedient. He understands, he settles down for another half-hour and then he again gives that small bark. 'Get up! Get up! The sun is high, and the paper boy has been.'

If I am late with his midday meal he stands and stares at the empty dish. When he wants water, he stares at the bowl, and if it is empty he overturns it and rattles it on the floor. He often has his meal outside, he prefers this for he takes out a piece of meat and puts it on the gravel for a last tit-bit. He cannot do that in the kitchen. Outside he often leaves a little food for the birds who wait watching him. Do they ask him 'Please leave a bit for a poor old beggar'? When he turns away they rush to the dish, perch on the edge and feast. He watches them with absorbed interest, but he never moves near to frighten them. One Scottie I had used to let the robin come between his paws as he lay watching the birds. Dirk shoos a bird away who comes too near, otherwise he seems to enjoy their chatter.

He is sympathetic. If his mistress is not well, or not in a good humour, he knows at once. When I am ill in bed he comes upstairs, puts his head round the door in a questioning way, then lies down by the side of the bed for an hour or so. Silently he steals away, leaving me to sleep. Then upstairs again he comes, and sadly surveys me.

He is polite, a gentleman of good manners. He never pushes or intrudes. I go first through a doorway, he waits for me. He is proud, and one cannot trick him. He doesn't like laughter that mocks him, but he enjoys a joke. Then he makes a sniffling sound, curls his lips and his eye twinkles as he sneezes. That sneeze is the essence of delight.

One Scottie, Hamish, an exceptionally clever dog, came running to me one morning, then running to the door and obviously he wanted me to follow him. I obeyed, he was in a hurry. Passing the house, on the opposite side of the road, was the smallest dog I have ever seen. A miniature creature, erect, perky, an exquisite little toy dog, with his mistress. My Scottie looked up at me, to see my reactions, then he wagged his tail and sneezed with laughter. We both laughed, enjoying the joke.

Dirk is loyal, and proud of me, he keeps an eye on me when I walk away and leave him in the car. He sits, watching for my return, sometimes in the driving seat with his paw on the steering wheel. One day he was left at the door of a house where I was calling. After a time the car hooter sounded. He sat there, with his paws on the hooter, looking surprised at his own effort.

His dark brown eyes sparkle, they are talking eyes, very beautiful, twinkling with fun, as he leaps about and dances, trying to persuade me to take him for a walk. I cannot resist, and he waits patiently for the lead, which unfortunately has to be used in this crowded town, where many dogs run loose and cause accidents.

A bone is his treasure; it is hidden in the garden and dug up when nobody is looking, for a quiet game on the lawn. He turns it to its rounded side, and rolls it, he holds it upright and bites, he licks it and admires it and then he leaves it for another time. Or he buries it, choosing the loose earth in the rock garden. Now I have a wire around this little garden of precious plants. This Scottie, unlike my other dogs, does not play ball. He runs after a ball but soon tires and refuses to play. His half-brother played ball from morning till night, and his mother was a ball-lover. This son of another dog has not the inherited zeal for rubber toys.

He enjoys the companionship of other small dogs, and we have a circle of friends—a lively little Corgi, called 'Bootie', with white socks, whom we meet and talk to in a road near. Dirk is keener on Bootie than he on Dirk.

Dirk excitedly pulls me towards the waiting dog who stands motionless, serene, uncaring as Dirk tries to rub noses. Dogs meet him at the gate, where he sits waiting each day to watch people pass. Does he think of the fields and woods where he might be, if there were no cars? He has never seen a rabbit, so he misses the joy of other Scotties who used to chase rabbits in the pastures. The grey squirrels give him great excitement as he chases after them when they come to the bird table. Cats are his bitter foes, and like all Scotties he races after them when he has the chance and sends them flying up a tree and away. I am not a cat-lover so I regard the flight without fear, for I know he cannot catch the quick creatures. He runs with ears laid flat, and his feet spin over the grass like a flash.

A dog's feet and paws fascinate me. I like to hold the small soft paws and tickle them. He walks so softly on the road, the sound of the tiny step is delicate and sweet to the ear. It is dainty, and beautiful, and in Autumn when the leaves fall he seems to enjoy walking through the leafy drifts under the beech trees, ruffling them up, sending them into a whirl as a child does.

This little Scottie has regular meals, not too much, and he has regular walks, along the same paths, for he seems to like something familiar. He is fit and well, and the best companion, a friend who never complains, who is never tiresome or stupid, a sensitive little person, giving love and faithful companionship. He has never been beaten, he is aware if he does wrong, and when he brings a bone into the house he looks at me, waiting to see what I do. I quietly put it outside and he goes out to eat in the garden.

Every Scottie is an individual, and quite different from other Scotties. Each Scottie seems to be the best ever known. His ears are pricked, alert, and he carries his tail like a black flag, upright and stiff, with a slight bend which is attractive. He is very strong, and he can break a rope or a leather lead if he objects to being fastened by it.

He doesn't mind the cold and he revels in snow, rolling in it and leaping through it in the early morning. He plays snowball, and catches the ball when I throw it. Although he seems impervious to cold weather Dirk wears a bright little coat in the winter. He is proud of it, and waits to have it buckled. Then out he walks, in his brown and scarlet-edged coat, to meet the babies in their prams or the dogs or postmen on the roads, to receive a word, a gesture, an admiring glance, and he stops and looks with affection at those who speak to him.

I think of Harold Monro's poem:

O little friend, your nose is ready; you sniff
Asking for that expected walk,
Your nostrils full of happy rabbit-whiff,
And almost talk.

Out through the garden, your head is already low,
You are going your walk you know,
And your limbs will draw
Joy from the earth through the touch of your padded
    paw.

I could wish for the return of the rabbits who made such fun in their wild skirmishes with other Scotties. I remember the dodging in and out of rabbit holes, and the way the rabbits teased my dog, popping into the earth and appearing behind him to his bewilderment. I could swear they enjoyed this hide-and-seek, once upon a time when the earth was richer in life.

It is not always realized that we human beings are honoured by the friendship of a dog, who is the only animal who accepts us and enters our lives, to dwell in our homes, to share our way of living. The cat remains a wild animal, it 'walks alone', it keeps its wild habits; the horse, closely allied to men, lives in a stable, not in our sitting-room and kitchens. A dog is obedient, he answers our call with alacrity, he follows our desires, staying quietly waiting like a patient child, enjoying a game, sleeping at the hours we sleep, waking with zest to a new day. He is faithful and humble, but proud of his master; he wishes to talk but no word can he utter, and his expressive eyes plead for understanding. Ever since the first wild dog followed man to a cave and joined his life to that of the human kind, deserting the pack and living in friendship with a two-legged resource-ful newly-evolving animal, the dog has been unique in the animal world.

PORTREE HIGH SCHOOL